DO WE ALL WANT THE SAME THING?

A COMPREHENSIVE CONFLICT RESOLUTION FRAMEWORK FOR EDUCATIONAL PROFESSIONALS

DR.OSCAR HARRIS

DISCLAIMER

This book is a work of general information and is not intended to provide specific advice or recommendations for any individual or on any specific security or investment product. It is only intended to provide education about the broader topic covered. The views and opinions expressed in this book are those of the author(s) and do not necessarily reflect the official policy or position of any agency of the author(s). Examples of analysis performed within this publication are only examples. They should not be utilized in real-world analytic products as they are based only on very limited and dated open source information.

While the publisher and author have made every effort to ensure the accuracy and completeness of the information contained in this book, we assume no responsibility for errors, inaccuracies, omissions, or any inconsistency herein. Any slights of people, places, or organizations are unintentional.

The publisher does not warrant that the information contained in this book is fully complete and shall not be responsible for any errors or omissions. The publisher and author shall have neither liability nor responsibility to any person or entity with respect to any loss or damage caused, or alleged to be caused, directly or indirectly by the information contained in this book.

FOREWORD

Welcome to a journey that explores the heart of understanding and resolving conflicts in our ever-changing world. This book takes you through the vibrant landscape of conflict resolution, touching on the essence of peace education, the impact of technology, and preparing for the conflicts of tomorrow. It's a guide designed for educators, students, and anyone eager to learn about transforming conflicts into opportunities for growth and understanding.

Through its pages, you'll discover innovative strategies such as mediation, negotiation, and active listening and insights illuminating the path to building more compassionate communities. This book is a beacon for those who believe in the power of empathy, dialogue, and cooperation. It encourages us to look beyond differences, find common ground, and work together towards a peaceful future.

TABLE OF CONTENTS

CHAPTER 1

UNDERSTANDING CONFLICT DYNAMICS

Conflict in schools is as inevitable as it is in any other social setting. It is characterized by a clash of interests, values, actions, or directions among students, teachers, administrators, or between these groups. This discord can emerge from a variety of sources: academic pressures, interpersonal relationships, behavioral issues, and differences in cultural, social, or personal backgrounds. Understanding the nature and definition of conflict within educational environments is pivotal for developing effective strategies to address and resolve these disagreements, ensuring a conducive learning atmosphere.

Fundamentally, conflict is an argument in which one or more participants feel that their needs, interests, or worries are at danger. This could manifest as a simple disagreement between students over group project roles in the school setting or as complex as disputes between the school administration and parents regarding policy implementations. Conflicts are not always destructive, despite the unfavorable perceptions they frequently carry. Instead, conflicts can serve as catalysts for change, providing opportunities for growth, learning, and improving existing systems and relationships when addressed constructively.

The dynamics of conflict in schools are influenced by the unique environment of educational institutions, where individuals from diverse backgrounds come together with the common goal of education and development. While this diversity is enriching, it also lays the groundwork for potential conflicts due to differences in opinions, beliefs, and values. Moreover, the hierarchical structure of schools, where authority is delineated among staff and students, adds another layer to conflict dynamics, influencing how disagreements are perceived and handled.

Identifying and understanding the types of conflicts common in schools is an essential first step toward resolution. Broadly, these conflicts can be categorized into interpersonal conflicts, intrapersonal conflicts, and structural conflicts. Interpersonal conflicts arise from interactions between individuals, such as bullying, harassment, or disputes among students or between students and teachers. Intrapersonal conflicts occur within an individual, often relating to self-esteem, identity, and personal goals, which can impact their behavior and interactions with others. Structural conflicts, for instance, could stem from the system and policies of the educational institution, including issues related to curriculum demands, assessment methods, and discipline policies. For example, a conflict might arise from a disagreement over the fairness of a particular assessment method or the strictness of a discipline policy.

Effective conflict resolution in schools requires a nuanced understanding of these complexities. It calls for strategies that address the immediate disagreement, consider the underlying causes, and work towards sustainable solutions. This entails creating an atmosphere that promotes empathy, respect, and candid communication among all members of the school community. By equipping students and staff with the skills to manage disagreements constructively, schools can transform potential conflicts into opportunities for positive change.

Moreover, implementing proactive measures, such as peer mediation programs, restorative justice practices (which focus on repairing the harm caused by conflict and restoring relationships), and conflict resolution education, can significantly reduce the occurrence and impact of conflicts. These approaches not only address conflicts as they arise but also work towards building a school culture that values understanding, collaboration, and mutual respect.

While school conflict is unavoidable, it does not have to disrupt the educational process. Understanding the nature and definition of conflict, along with its potential causes and types, is crucial for managing disagreements effectively. By using efficient conflict resolution strategies, schools may foster an environment that promotes learning, individual growth, and positive relationships among all members of the educational community. This holistic approach to conflict management underscores the importance of addressing disagreements' symptoms and root causes, ensuring a harmonious and productive learning environment for everyone involved.

The Psychological Needs Leading to Conflicts

Conflicts in schools often stem from the unmet psychological needs of students, educators, and administrative staff. Understanding these needs is essential for creating an environment that minimizes conflicts and fosters a nurturing educational atmosphere. Psychological needs, as identified by various theories of human motivation and behavior, include the need for belonging, esteem, autonomy, and competence. When these needs are not satisfied, individuals may experience frustration, anxiety, or aggression, leading to conflicts within the school environment.

The need for belonging represents the human desire to be accepted and valued by others. This need manifests in students' and educators' pursuit of forming meaningful connections with peers and colleagues in schools. When students feel isolated or rejected by their peers or overlooked by their teachers, or when educators feel disconnected from their students or colleagues, the resultant sense of alienation can breed conflicts. Bullying, exclusion, and

13

cliques are direct manifestations of thwarted belonging needs, leading to interpersonal conflicts among students. At the same time, a lack of collaboration or support among staff can create a divisive atmosphere.

Esteem needs refer to the desire for respect, recognition, and accomplishment. Students and educators alike strive for acknowledgment of their efforts and achievements. When these needs are unmet, it can lead to feelings of inadequacy and resentment. For students, constant academic pressure without recognition, comparison with peers, or punitive disciplinary measures can lead to behavioral issues and conflicts with authority figures. For educators, a lack of professional development opportunities, peer acknowledgment, or support from the administration can result in job dissatisfaction and disputes within the workplace.

Autonomy needs to involve the desire for freedom and control over one's life. In the educational setting, students often face conflicts when they feel their voices are unheard or when rigid school rules or authoritative figures overly control them. Similarly, educators experience conflicts when they perceive a need for more agency in their teaching methods or decision-making processes within the school's administration. Conflicts arising from unmet autonomy needs can manifest as power struggles, resistance to authority, and defiance, undermining the educational process.

Competence needs are centered around the desire to be effective in dealing with the environment, to master tasks, and to gain knowledge and skills. In schools, students may conflict when they encounter academic challenges without adequate support, leading to frustration and avoidance behaviors. Educators facing unrealistic expectations from the administration, parents, or standardized testing pressures may feel incompetent, triggering job performance and satisfaction conflicts.

Addressing the psychological needs leading to conflicts requires a holistic approach that recognizes the diverse needs of all school community members. Implementing strategies such as creating a supportive and inclusive school culture, recognizing and celebrating achievements, providing opportunities for student and staff input, and offering support for skill development can help meet these psychological needs. Additionally, fostering an environment that encourages empathy, understanding, and open communication can mitigate the impact of unmet needs and prevent the escalation of conflicts.

By recognizing and managing the mental health requirements of both teachers and students, educational institutions can foster a constructive and cooperative learning atmosphere. This proactive approach not only prevents conflicts but also enhances the well-being and satisfaction of all school community members, ultimately contributing to a more effective and enriching educational experience.

Types of Conflicts: Interpersonal, Intrapersonal, and Institutional

Understanding the conflicts within schools is crucial for implementing effective resolution strategies. Broadly categorized, conflicts in educational settings manifest as interpersonal, intrapersonal, and institutional. Each type stems from distinct sources and requires tailored approaches for resolution, underscoring the complexity of managing discord in such diverse environments.

Interpersonal Conflicts are the most visible type within schools, occurring between two or more individuals. These conflicts can arise from misunderstandings, personality clashes, competition, or differing values and beliefs. In school, interpersonal conflicts are commonly seen among students, such as disputes over social dynamics, bullying, or academic collaboration. However, they also occur among staff members or between students and teachers, often stemming from communication breakdowns, workload distribution, or disciplinary measures. Addressing these conflicts effectively requires improving communication, empathy, and understanding between the parties involved. Strategies like mediation, active listening exercises, and collaborative problem-solving can help rebuild relationships and find mutually agreeable solutions.

Intrapersonal Conflicts involve a conflict within an individual, reflecting a struggle with self-esteem, identity, goals, or emotional regulation. For students, these conflicts might relate to academic pressures, future aspirations, or social belonging, leading to stress, anxiety, or disengagement from school activities. Educators, too, may experience intrapersonal conflicts, grappling with professional identity, work-life balance, or ethical dilemmas. Resolving intrapersonal conflicts requires introspection and self-awareness, often facilitated by counseling, mentorship, or support groups. Educational institutions can support individuals facing such conflicts by providing resources for mental health, creating safe spaces for expression, and fostering a culture that encourages personal growth and self-compassion.

Institutional Conflicts arise from the educational institution's policies, structures, and culture. These conflicts can be related to curriculum choices, resource allocation, school governance, or the implementation of rules and regulations. Often, institutional conflicts reflect broader disagreements over educational philosophies, equity, and inclusion, or the balance between discipline and autonomy. Addressing institutional conflicts demands a systemic approach that involves stakeholder engagement, policy review, and, at times, organizational change. Creating forums for dialogue, conducting needs assessments, and involving diverse voices in decision-making processes can help reconcile differing views and align school practices with the needs and values of the school community.

Recognizing the types of conflicts—interpersonal, intrapersonal, and institutional—allows educational leaders, teachers, and students to apply targeted conflict resolution strategies. By understanding these conflicts' underlying causes and dynamics, schools can implement effective interventions that address the root issues, promote healing, and prevent future discord. Cultivating an environment that proactively addresses these diverse conflicts enhances the educational experience. It prepares students with the skills to navigate challenges in their personal and professional lives beyond the school setting.

The Role of Communication in Conflict Emergence

The emergence of conflicts within educational settings often has its roots in communication or, more precisely, the lack thereof or its mismanagement. Communication—the exchange of information, ideas, feelings, and values—serves as the lifeblood of any social interaction, particularly in the complex ecosystem of a school. However, when communication falters through misunderstanding, omission, or distortion, it can become a potent catalyst for conflict. Recognizing and resolving the fundamental problems that give rise to conflicts requires an understanding of communication's role in the process.

Misunderstandings arise as one of the most common precursors to conflict, stemming from unclear, incomplete, or misinterpreted messages. In the hustle of school life, instructions can be rushed, and intentions can be misread, leading to confusion and frustration among students and educators alike. A teacher's offhand remark might be interpreted as a personal slight by a student; similarly, a student's question might be perceived as challenging authority, setting the stage for interpersonal conflicts rooted in miscommunication.

The absence of communication, or silence, also plays a significant role in conflict emergence. Issues left unaddressed, whether due to avoidance, fear of confrontation, or assumption that others should "just know," can fester, creating a breeding ground for resentment and misunderstanding. In schools where the stakes of social and academic performance are high, the reluctance to express concerns or ask for help can lead to significant intrapersonal and interpersonal conflicts, from academic stress to bullying.

Moreover, the mode and tone of communication significantly impact conflict emergence. Aggressive or passive-aggressive communication styles can escalate disputes, while passive communication might lead to unresolved issues and dissatisfaction. Digital communication platforms, while facilitating information exchange, often need more nuances of face-to-face interaction, such as tone and body language, leading to increased potential for misunderstandings among students and staff.

Furthermore, the cultural context of communication must be considered. Schools are melting pots of diverse cultures, each with its communication norms and values. What is regarded as a straightforward manner of speaking in one culture might be perceived as rude in another. These cultural misunderstandings can lead to conflicts that stem from a need for more awareness and sensitivity toward different communication styles and expectations.

Schools must foster an environment that prioritizes clear, compassionate, and culturally sensitive communication to mitigate the role of communication in conflict emergence. To do this, instructors and students must get training in practical communication skills, including assertiveness, empathy, active listening, and the responsible use of digital communication tools. Establishing open channels for feedback and dialogue, encouraging reflective communication practices, and celebrating cultural diversity can also significantly prevent conflicts.

Understanding how communication plays a critical part in the genesis of conflict, educational institutions should take proactive measures to address the underlying reasons for disagreements. Cultivating a culture of open, respectful, and effective communication minimizes the potential for conflict. It enhances the educational experience, creating a community where every member feels heard, understood, and valued.

Recognizing and Addressing the Root Causes of Conflicts

Addressing conflicts effectively in educational settings extends beyond managing immediate disagreements. It requires delving into the root causes of conflicts, which are often complex, multifaceted, and deeply embedded within the school environment's interactions and structures. Recognizing and addressing these underlying issues are crucial steps toward fostering a harmonious educational community and preventing the recurrence of similar disputes.

The root causes of school conflicts can vary widely, but they often include unmet needs, perceived inequalities, cultural misunderstandings, and structural or systemic issues. Unmet needs, whether emotional, social, or academic, can lead to frustration and isolation among students and staff, manifesting as conflicts. Perceived inequalities, whether in access to resources, attention, or opportunities, can create a sense of injustice and competition, fueling disputes among individuals and groups.

Due to the varied values, beliefs, and communication methods within the school community, miscommunications and disputes might result from cultural misunderstandings. Structural or systemic issues, such as rigid policies or inadequate support systems, can exacerbate individual and collective stresses, leading to organizational disputes.

Recognizing these root causes requires a proactive and attentive approach. It involves listening actively to all parties' concerns, observing interactions and dynamics within the school, and gathering information through formal and informal channels. Surveys, feedback sessions, and open forums can be valuable tools for uncovering the underlying issues that fuel conflicts.

Addressing the root causes of conflicts necessitates a strategic and holistic approach. Schools can implement support systems for unmet needs, such as counseling services, peer support groups, and extracurricular activities, to provide outlets and assistance for students and staff. In order to promote justice and equity in the allocation of resources, opportunities, and recognition, policies and procedures pertaining to perceived inequities may need to be reviewed and revised.

To overcome cultural misunderstandings, schools can foster a culture of diversity and inclusion through education, celebration of cultural events, and training on intercultural communication and empathy. Addressing structural or systemic issues may require more extensive organizational changes, including policy revisions, introducing new support mechanisms, and enhancing communication channels within the school.

Moreover, it is essential to empower the school community to participate in identifying and addressing root causes. This can be achieved through establishing committees or working groups, involving students, staff, and parents in decision-making processes, and providing platforms for sharing ideas and solutions. Such collaborative efforts contribute to resolving the underlying conflicts and foster a sense of ownership and commitment to the school's well-being among all stakeholders.

Recognizing and addressing the root causes of conflicts in educational settings is critical to creating a positive and supportive environment conducive to learning and growth. By taking a proactive, inclusive, and strategic approach, schools can transform potential areas of dispute into opportunities for improvement, collaboration, and enhanced understanding among all school community members. This foundational work lays the groundwork for long-term peace and harmony within the educational landscape, where every individual has the opportunity to thrive.

The Impact of Conflict on the Educational Environment

Conflicts within educational settings can have profound and far-reaching impacts on the academic environment, affecting students, educators, and the broader school community. Human interaction will inevitably lead to conflict, but how it is handled can significantly impact how it turns out. Unresolved or poorly managed conflicts can lead to a hostile atmosphere, whereas effectively addressed disputes can foster a sense of resilience and community.

One of the most immediate impacts of conflict is disrupting the learning environment. Disputes among students or between students and teachers can consume significant classroom time and divert attention away from educational objectives. The emotional turmoil can lead to decreased concentration, lowered academic performance, and absenteeism for students directly involved in a conflict. Similarly, educators embroiled in conflicts may experience stress and burnout, which can diminish their effectiveness in the classroom and lead to a lack of enthusiasm for teaching.

Beyond the classroom, conflicts can erode the sense of community within a school. Interpersonal disputes can fracture student groups, leading to polarization and cliques that exclude and isolate individuals. Such divisions can inhibit the development of a supportive, cohesive school culture, making it difficult for students to feel a sense of belonging. For educators and staff, conflicts can create a tense working environment where collaboration and communication are hindered by mistrust and resentment.

The emotional well-being of students and staff is another area significantly impacted by conflict. Persistent or intense disputes can contribute to feelings of anxiety, depression, and low self-esteem among students. The stress associated with unresolved conflicts can also affect physical health, manifesting as headaches, fatigue, and other stress-related ailments. Educators are not immune to these effects; ongoing conflicts can lead to professional dissatisfaction and impact personal well-being.

Furthermore, conflicts can undermine respect for authority and the overall discipline within the school. Students may grow disenchanted with school administration and rules if they witness adult issues being mishandled or perceive that their complaints are ignored or poorly handled. This disillusionment can lead to increased behavioral problems and challenges to school rules, further destabilizing the educational environment.

However, it's essential to recognize that conflict, when addressed constructively, can also have positive impacts. It can catalyze change, prompting reviewing and improving policies, practices, and relationships. Conflicts can stimulate dialogue and debate, leading to a deeper understanding of diverse perspectives and developing students' critical thinking and negotiation skills. For educators, effectively navigating conflicts can enhance professional growth and strengthen team dynamics.

To mitigate conflict's negative impacts and harness its potential for positive change, schools must adopt comprehensive conflict resolution strategies. These strategies include promoting open communication, fostering empathy and understanding, and training students and staff in conflict resolution skills. To address the underlying causes of conflicts and mend relationships, restorative practices, peer mediation programs, and supportive counseling services must also be implemented.

The impact of conflict on the educational environment underscores the importance of proactive and effective conflict management. By cultivating a school culture that values respect, inclusivity, and open dialogue, academic institutions can minimize the detrimental effects of conflicts and create a more supportive, engaging, and enriching learning experience for all members of the school community.

Strategies for Early Detection and Prevention of Conflicts

In the intricate landscape of educational environments, early detection and prevention of conflicts are crucial strategies for maintaining harmony and promoting a conducive learning atmosphere. By identifying potential sources of discord before they escalate and implementing preventative measures, schools can significantly enhance the educational experience for both students and educators. This approach addresses conflicts at their nascent stage and fosters a culture of proactive problem-solving and mutual respect.

Early Detection of Conflicts

1. Open Lines of Communication: Encouraging open and honest communication within the school community is fundamental. Establishing a setting in which employees and students feel free to voice complaints and issues can aid in the early detection of disputes. Regular meetings, suggestion boxes, and open-door policies with teachers and administrators are practical tools for fostering dialogue.

2. Observant Educators and Staff: Teachers and staff members who are attuned to the dynamics of their students and colleagues play a pivotal role in early conflict detection. It might be helpful to discover underlying difficulties before they become more serious by teaching educators to spot the warning signals of distress, which include changes in behavior, academic performance, or social interactions.

3. Peer Monitoring: Implementing peer monitoring programs where students are trained to identify and report conflicts among their peers can be an effective strategy. These initiatives give students the tools they need to actively contribute to preserving a pleasant school climate and can offer insightful perspectives on the student body.

4. Surveys and Feedback Mechanisms: Regularly conducting anonymous surveys or feedback sessions can provide valuable information about the school climate and potential conflict areas. This data-driven approach allows administrators to identify trends and issues that may not be visible on the surface.

Prevention of Conflicts

5. Conflict Resolution Education: Integrating conflict resolution education into the curriculum equips students with the skills to manage disputes constructively. Teaching strategies such as active listening, empathy, negotiation, and mediation encourage students to resolve disagreements amicably and understand the importance of perspective-taking.

6. Promoting a Positive School Culture: Conflict avoidance requires fostering an environment in schools that values inclusivity, diversity, and respect. Celebrating different cultures, hosting team-building activities, and reinforcing positive behavior can help build a sense of community and reduce the likelihood of disputes.

7. Proactive Policies and Procedures: Developing clear policies and procedures for handling conflicts sets a standard for behavior and conflict management within the school. These guidelines should be communicated clearly to all school community members and should emphasize restorative practices over punitive measures.

8. Professional Development for Educators: Providing educators with ongoing professional development in conflict detection, prevention, and resolution ensures they have the tools and knowledge to effectively address disputes. Training can cover various topics, including communication techniques, cultural competency, and stress management.

9. Mental Health Support: Recognizing the link between mental health and conflicts, schools should provide accessible mental health resources for students and staff. Support groups, health initiatives, and counseling services can all help with the psychological and emotional aspects of conflict.

10. Engaging Parents and Guardians: Building strong partnerships with parents and guardians can play a significant role in conflict prevention. Keeping parents informed about school policies, student progress, and available resources fosters a collaborative approach to addressing potential issues.

By adopting these strategies for the early detection and prevention of conflicts, schools can create a nurturing environment where educational goals are achieved without disruption. These efforts contribute to the immediate well-being of the school community and equip students with lifelong skills in conflict management, empathy, and cooperation.

CHAPTER 2

PREPARING FOR CONFLICT RESOLUTION

Establishing a safe and neutral environment for dialogue is a fundamental step in addressing and resolving conflicts within educational settings. This approach ensures that all parties feel valued, heard, and respected, setting the stage for constructive conversations and developing mutually agreeable solutions. A well-designed setting promotes the school community's general wellbeing and cohesiveness while aiding in the resolution process. Here are key considerations and strategies for creating such an environment:

1. Physical Space: Choosing an appropriate physical location is crucial. The space should be private, comfortable, and away from school life's daily hustle and bustle. Neutral ground, where no party feels at a disadvantage or overly scrutinized, helps minimize power dynamics. A bright, well-ventilated, and arranged in a circle or semi-circle room encourages open communication and equality among participants.

2. Psychological Safety: Beyond the physical aspects, the environment must be psychologically safe. This means creating an atmosphere where individuals feel secure enough to express their thoughts and emotions without fear of judgment, retaliation, or dismissal. Establishing ground rules at the start of the dialogue can aid in this. These rules include confidentiality, respect for all opinions, and a commitment to listen actively.

3. Facilitation: Having a neutral facilitator to guide the conversation is often beneficial. This individual, possibly a trained mediator, counselor, or a respected educator not directly involved in the conflict, can ensure that the discussion remains focused, respectful, and productive. They can also assist in controlling emotions and step in if the discussion goes off course or is hostile.

4. Preparation: Before engaging in dialogue, all parties should be mentally and emotionally prepared. This might involve preliminary meetings with the facilitator to set intentions, outline concerns, and discuss hopes for the outcome. Such preparation helps participants approach the dialogue with a constructive mindset, ready to engage in meaningful exchange.

5. Encouragement of Active Listening: Active listening should be a cornerstone of the dialogue process. Encouraging participants to listen attentively, reflect on what they hear, and ask clarifying questions promotes understanding and empathy. This practice can help de-escalate emotions and illuminate the underlying issues contributing to the conflict.

6. Respect for Diverse Perspectives: Recognizing and valuing the diversity of experiences and viewpoints is essential. A safe and neutral environment is one where differences are seen as opportunities for learning rather than sources of division. This perspective encourages participants to be open to new insights and consider solutions accommodating various needs.

7. Commitment to Action: The dialogue should aim towards actionable outcomes. While creating a safe and neutral environment for conversation is vital, the ultimate goal is to resolve the conflict constructively. This requires a commitment from all parties to work towards agreed-upon actions, follow-up meetings, and ongoing support if needed.

By meticulously establishing a safe and neutral environment for dialogue, schools can effectively navigate the complexities of conflicts, turning challenges into opportunities for growth and learning. Such efforts address the immediate issues at hand and contribute to building a school culture characterized by open communication, respect, and resilience.

The Importance of Active Listening and Empathy in Conflict Resolution

Active listening and empathy are indispensable in conflict resolution, especially in educational environments. These skills transcend mere conversation techniques; they represent a commitment to genuinely understanding the perspectives and emotions of all parties involved. Their importance cannot be overstated, as they lay the groundwork for building trust, fostering mutual respect, and facilitating the collaborative exploration of solutions to conflicts.

Active Listening: A Pathway to Understanding

Active listening involves:

- Giving full attention to the speaker.
- Reflecting on what has been said.
- Responding thoughtfully.

In the context of conflict resolution, it serves several crucial functions. First, it validates the speaker's feelings and experiences, conveying that their perspective is essential and worthy of consideration. This validation can be incredibly soothing and is often the first step towards de-escalating a tense situation.

Moreover, active listening aids in uncovering the underlying issues fueling the conflict. School conflicts often manifest as surface-level disputes but stem from deeper concerns or unmet needs. Through active listening, participants can move beyond the conflict's symptoms to understand its root causes, paving the way for more effective and sustainable resolutions.

Additionally, active listening involves summarizing and paraphrasing the speaker's words, ensuring clarity and mutual understanding. This practice minimizes misunderstandings and assumptions that can exacerbate conflicts, promoting a clear and shared comprehension of the issues.

Empathy: The Heart of Connection

Empathy is synonymous with active listening. It involves putting oneself in another's shoes and understanding their feelings and perspectives from their viewpoint. In conflict resolution, empathy transforms interactions by fostering a sense of shared humanity and concern for each other's well-being.

Empathy has the power to dissolve barriers of defensiveness and resentment. When individuals feel genuinely understood, they are more likely to drop their guard and become open to considering alternative viewpoints and solutions. Empathy also encourages compassion and kindness, which are essential for healing and rebuilding relationships after conflicts.

Furthermore, demonstrating empathy in conflict resolution sends a powerful message about the value of emotional intelligence and respect for others. It models positive behavior for students and teaches them invaluable life skills about how to interact with others in a considerate and constructive manner.

Integrating Active Listening and Empathy in Conflict Resolution

To effectively incorporate active listening and empathy into conflict resolution processes, schools can undertake several initiatives. Training sessions for students, teachers, and administrators on these skills can be immensely beneficial, providing practical techniques and opportunities for practice.

Creating guidelines and structures that promote empathetic communication and active listening during conflict resolution meetings or mediations can also help institutionalize these practices. Additionally, integrating these concepts into the curriculum as part of social-emotional learning programs ensures that students develop these skills early.

Recognizing and celebrating instances where active listening and empathy lead to successful conflict resolution can further reinforce their value. Highlighting these successes through school communications or assemblies can inspire the school community to embrace these approaches.

Active listening and empathy are not just conflict resolution strategies but foundational elements for nurturing a supportive, respectful, and cohesive school environment. By prioritizing these skills, educational institutions can address conflicts more effectively and cultivate a culture that values understanding, compassion, and collaboration.

Setting Clear Goals and Objectives for Conflict Resolution Processes

Setting clear goals and objectives for conflict resolution processes is pivotal in guiding the direction and outcomes of these engagements within educational settings. This structured approach ensures that all parties understand what they hope to achieve, making the process more focused, efficient, and effective. Establishing these targets early on helps to navigate the complexities of conflicts with a sense of purpose and direction, ultimately facilitating more constructive and meaningful resolutions.

Defining the Purpose of Resolution

Clearly defining the goal of the conflict resolution process is the first step towards establishing goals and objectives. Is the aim merely to resolve a disagreement, or is it to rebuild a damaged relationship? Understanding the broader purpose helps frame the subsequent steps and ensures that the solutions identified are aligned with the desired outcomes. For instance, if the goal is to mend a relationship, the process may prioritize open communication and empathy beyond addressing the immediate issue.

Identifying Specific Objectives

Once the overarching purpose is established, the next step involves identifying specific, actionable objectives. These should be concrete, measurable, and attainable, providing a roadmap for the conflict resolution process. Objectives may include:

- Establishing mutual respect among parties.
- Developing a shared understanding of the conflict's root causes.
- Agreeing on specific behavioral changes.
- Implementing ongoing communication and feedback mechanisms.

Articulating these objectives sets the stage for a focused discussion and targeted problem-solving.

Collaborative Goal Setting

Involving all parties in the goal-setting process is crucial for ensuring buy-in and commitment to conflict resolution. Collaborative goal-setting empowers individuals by giving them a voice and enhances the likelihood of achieving sustainable outcomes. Through dialogue and negotiation, parties can reconcile differing views and agree on common goals, fostering a cooperative rather than adversarial approach to conflict resolution.

Flexibility and Adaptability

While clear goals and objectives are essential, flexibility and adaptability should also be incorporated into the process. Conflicts are dynamic; unexpected issues or insights may arise during resolution discussions. Being open to adjusting goals as needed ensures that the process remains relevant and responsive to the conflict's evolving nature and the parties' needs.

Monitoring Progress towards Goals

Establishing mechanisms for monitoring progress towards the set goals is critical to conflict resolution. This may involve regular check-ins, feedback sessions, or the use of specific indicators to assess whether the objectives are being met. Monitoring progress allows course correction if needed, reinforces accountability, and ensures that the resolution process maintains momentum.

Revisiting Goals Post-Resolution

Finally, revisiting the goals and objectives after resolving the conflict can provide valuable insights for future conflict management efforts. This reflective practice allows parties to evaluate the effectiveness of the resolution process, learn from the experience, and identify areas for improvement. It also reinforces the importance of setting clear goals and objectives in achieving meaningful and lasting resolutions to conflicts.

Setting clear goals and objectives is foundational to effective conflict resolution in educational environments. This approach clarifies the direction and purpose of the resolution efforts and ensures that all parties are aligned in their expectations and commitments. By prioritizing collaborative, flexible, and focused goal setting, schools can navigate conflicts more effectively, leading to more positive outcomes for students, educators, and the broader school community.

Selecting Appropriate Conflict Resolution Strategies

Selecting appropriate conflict resolution strategies is critical in navigating the complex dynamics of disputes within educational settings. The effectiveness of the resolution process heavily depends on choosing strategies aligned with the nature of the conflict, the needs of the involved parties, and the overarching goals of the educational institution. This tailored approach ensures that disputes are not just superficially managed but are resolved to promote understanding, growth, and long-term harmony.

Understanding the Conflict

Before selecting a resolution strategy, it's essential to understand the conflict at hand thoroughly. This involves analyzing the causes of the dispute, the parties involved, and the conflict's impact on the educational environment. Whether the conflict is interpersonal, involving disagreements between students or staff, or institutional, stemming from systemic issues within the school, understanding the nuances of the conflict is the first step toward effective resolution.

Tailoring Strategies to the Conflict Type

Peer mediation and mediation may be the most successful approaches for resolving interpersonal issues because they allow the parties to engage in direct dialogue and negotiation. For intrapersonal conflicts, counseling or coaching can provide individuals with the support and tools to address internal struggles and how they manifest in disputes with others. When dealing with institutional conflicts, open forums, policy reviews, or task forces may be more appropriate to address the systemic issues at play.

Fostering Open Communication

Regardless of the selected strategy, fostering open and respectful communication is foundational to any effective conflict-resolution process. Strategies that encourage dialogue, such as restorative circles or facilitated discussions, can help bridge misunderstandings, clarify perspectives, and build empathy among the parties involved. Creating a safe space for honest expression is crucial for moving toward resolution.

Incorporating Restorative Practices

Rather than penalizing misbehavior, restorative methods emphasize relationship restoration and harm healing. In the educational context, these practices can include restorative conversations, agreements, or circles that involve not just the conflicting parties but also other community members who may have been affected. This approach addresses the immediate conflict and works towards building a stronger, more cohesive school community.

Prioritizing Emotional Intelligence

Strategies that prioritize developing and applying emotional intelligence can be particularly effective in resolving conflicts. Training sessions or workshops focusing on understanding emotions, empathetic listening, and managing stress can equip students and educators with the skills they need to navigate disputes constructively. Emotional intelligence fosters a school environment where conflicts are less likely to escalate and more likely to be resolved positively.

Engaging in Collaborative Problem-Solving

Working collaboratively to determine the fundamental needs of each party and coming up with solutions that address those needs is the process of collaborative problem-solving. This strategy emphasizes the importance of cooperation over competition and seeks win-win outcomes. By involving all parties in the resolution process, collaborative problem-solving can lead to more sustainable and satisfactory resolutions.

Monitoring and Adjusting Strategies

Finally, it's essential to recognize that conflict resolution is ongoing. Strategies should be monitored for effectiveness and adjusted based on feedback and outcomes. This iterative approach allows schools to continually refine their conflict resolution processes and respond to conflicts with increasing efficacy over time.

In selecting appropriate conflict resolution strategies, schools must take a deliberate and informed approach that considers the unique characteristics of each conflict and the needs of their community. Education institutions can settle disagreements in a way that solves the present problem and promotes a healthy and encouraging learning environment by customizing tactics to the particular situation, encouraging open communication, and placing a high priority on the restoration of relationships.

Engaging All Parties in the Conflict Resolution Process

Engaging all parties in the conflict resolution process is essential to effectively addressing disputes within educational settings. This inclusive approach ensures that each individual involved has the opportunity to contribute their perspective, fostering a sense of ownership and commitment to the resolution. When all parties are actively involved, the solutions developed are more likely to be comprehensive, equitable, and sustainable, ultimately leading to a more harmonious educational environment.

Building Trust and Willingness to Participate

The initial step in engaging all parties is establishing trust and a willingness to participate in the resolution process. This can be achieved by ensuring confidentiality, demonstrating impartiality, and communicating the benefits of active involvement. Educators and conflict resolution facilitators can set the tone by being open, respectful, and empathetic, creating an atmosphere where participants feel safe and valued.

Acknowledging and Valuing Diverse Perspectives

Recognizing the importance of diverse perspectives is crucial for effective conflict resolution. Each party involved brings their own experiences, beliefs, and emotions to the table. By acknowledging and valuing these differences, the resolution process becomes an opportunity for learning and growth. Facilitators can encourage participants to express their views fully and listen to others openly, promoting understanding and empathy among the conflicting parties.

Facilitating Open Communication

Open communication is the cornerstone of engaging all parties in the conflict resolution process. Facilitators can employ various techniques to ensure effective dialogue, such as active listening exercises, "I" statements to express feelings and needs without blame, and structured turn-taking to ensure everyone has the chance to speak. Creating an environment where participants feel heard and understood can contribute to finding common ground.

Implementing Collaborative Problem-Solving Techniques

Collaborative problem-solving is a strategy that emphasizes working together to identify issues, generate solutions, and agree on a course of action. This method, which is supported by guiding questions, brainstorming sessions, and consensus-building exercises, calls for the active involvement of all stakeholders. Through collaboration, participants can develop solutions that reflect a shared understanding of the conflict and a mutual commitment to resolving it.

Providing Support and Resources

It is crucial to provide participants with support throughout the conflict resolution process, particularly when there are strong feelings involved or the problems are very complicated. Providing access to counseling services, offering communication and negotiation skills workshops, and ensuring participants have the necessary information and resources can help maintain engagement and momentum toward resolution.

Ensuring Representation and Inclusivity

Ensuring that all voices are represented, especially those of marginalized or less vocal participants, is vital for a fair and inclusive resolution process. This may involve reaching out to individuals who are reluctant to participate, offering various modes of participation to accommodate different needs, and being attentive to power dynamics that inhibit open expression.

Reflecting and Learning from the Process

Finally, engaging all parties in conflict resolution is an opportunity for reflection and learning. After reaching the resolution, participants can benefit from discussing what worked well, what challenges were encountered, and how the process could be improved. This reflective practice reinforces the lessons learned and strengthens the community's capacity to address future conflicts more effectively.

Engaging all parties in the conflict resolution process is a dynamic and participatory approach that values the contributions of each individual involved. Educational institutions can navigate conflicts with greater empathy, equity, and effectiveness by building trust, facilitating open communication, and employing collaborative problem-solving. This collective journey resolves the immediate issues and fosters a stronger, more connected school community.

Gathering and Analyzing Relevant Information

Gathering and analyzing relevant information is a pivotal step in conflict resolution in educational settings. Through a systematic process, educators, administrators, and conflict resolution facilitators may comprehend the extent and intricacy of the argument and arrive at informed selections that tackle the root causes instead of merely treating the symptoms. A comprehensive knowledge of the situation lays the groundwork for developing effective, sustainable solutions tailored to the conflict's specific dynamics.

Collecting Comprehensive Information

The first step involves collecting information from various sources to ensure a complete understanding of the conflict. This can include direct accounts from the involved parties, observations from teachers or staff who may have witnessed the conflict or its effects, and relevant documentation such as emails, notes, or school reports. Involving diverse perspectives is crucial for obtaining a balanced view of the situation, highlighting that conflicts often have multiple facets and may be perceived differently by each participant.

Employing Active Listening

Active listening plays a critical role in gathering information. Facilitators can uncover underlying issues that may not be immediately apparent by engaging in empathetic listening and encouraging open and honest communication. This involves paying attention to what is said and noting non-verbal cues and emotions that might indicate deeper concerns. Participants are more willing to openly share their experiences and points of view when there is an atmosphere of trust and respect fostered by active listening.

Utilizing Surveys and Questionnaires

Surveys and questionnaires can be practical tools for gathering information, especially in cases where direct dialogue may be challenging or when seeking to understand the broader context of the conflict. These resources can offer insightful information about a more comprehensive community's beliefs, attitudes, and experiences, which can help spot any patterns or trends that might fuel the dispute.

Conducting Conflict Analysis

Once the information has been gathered, the next step is to analyze it to identify the key issues, needs, and interests of the parties involved. Conflict analysis consists of looking beyond the immediate dispute to understand the broader context, including any historical factors, power dynamics, and external influences that may be at play. This analysis helps clarify the conflict's root causes, which is essential for developing effective resolution strategies.

Mapping the Conflict

Creating a visual conflict map can help organize and interpret the information gathered. This might include identifying the main parties involved, the issues at stake, the relationships between parties, and any patterns of interaction. A conflict map provides a clear overview of the situation, making it easier to identify potential areas for intervention and communicate the conflict's complexities to others.

Prioritizing Issues

Not all issues identified in the analysis will have the same importance or urgency. Prioritizing matters based on their impact on the parties involved and the educational environment allows facilitators to focus their efforts where they are most needed. This prioritization should be done in consultation with the involved parties, ensuring their perspectives and needs are considered.

Developing a Resolution Strategy

After thoroughly understanding the conflict through gathering and analyzing information, the final step is to develop a resolution strategy that addresses the identified needs and issues. This strategy should be tailored to the specific context of the conflict, considering the most effective approaches for the individuals and issues involved. It may include a combination of direct negotiation, mediation, restorative practices, or other conflict resolution methods.

Gathering and analyzing relevant information is a meticulous process that requires patience, empathy, and a commitment to understanding the full scope of the conflict. By undertaking this process with diligence and care, educators and facilitators can develop informed, nuanced approaches to conflict resolution that promote healing, understanding, and positive change within the educational setting.

Building Trust among Conflict Parties

Building trust among conflict parties is fundamental to resolving disputes within educational environments. Trust forms the bedrock of constructive dialogue and collaboration, allowing conflicting parties to approach resolution with openness and a willingness to understand each other's perspectives. Without trust, the resolution process would become mired in skepticism and resistance, hindering any meaningful progress. Establishing and nurturing trust requires intentional efforts from educators, administrators, and conflict resolution facilitators, who must model trustworthiness and foster an atmosphere where trust can flourish.

Demonstrating Consistency and Reliability

Trust is cultivated when individuals demonstrate consistency and reliability in their actions and words. For educators and facilitators involved in conflict resolution, this means following through on promises, maintaining confidentiality, and adhering to established procedures and principles. By being consistent in their approach and reliable in their commitments, they signal to all parties involved that they can be trusted to manage the process fairly and effectively.

Facilitating Open and Honest Communication

Establishing channels of open and honest communication is essential to fostering trust. This entails empowering everyone to voice their ideas, emotions, and worries without worrying about criticism or backlash. Facilitators can support this process by establishing clear ground rules for communication, actively listening to what is being said, and validating the experiences of each participant. By fostering an environment where individuals feel heard and respected, trust begins to take root.

Acknowledging and Valuing Each Party's Perspective

Trust grows when individuals feel that their perspectives are acknowledged and valued. In conflict situations, facilitators must recognize the validity of each party's viewpoint, even when they differ. This doesn't mean agreeing with everyone but rather affirming that each perspective is an essential piece of the puzzle. When parties see their views taken seriously, they are more likely to trust and engage with the resolution process constructively.

Promoting Transparency

Transparency in the conflict resolution process is critical to building trust. This means communicating the process steps, the rationale behind decisions, and any potential limitations or challenges. Facilitators can preempt misunderstandings and skepticism by being transparent, creating a sense of security and confidence among the conflicting parties.

Modeling Respectful Behavior

Trust is also nurtured through the modeling of respectful behavior. Facilitators and educators must lead by example, treating each party with dignity and respect, regardless of the circumstances. This includes using respectful language, avoiding taking sides, and showing patience and understanding. When respect is consistently demonstrated, it sets a positive tone for interactions and encourages trust among all participants.

Encouraging Shared Experiences

Shared experiences can serve as a powerful tool for building trust. Facilitators might consider organizing activities or dialogues that allow conflicting parties to work together towards a common goal or to share personal experiences related to the conflict. These shared experiences can break down barriers, highlight commonalities, and foster a sense of camaraderie and trust.

Rebuilding Trust after Setbacks

Finally, it's essential to recognize that building trust is an ongoing process that may experience setbacks. When trust is harmed—whether by a mistake, a misunderstanding, or a breach of confidentiality—it is imperative to address the matter head-on and take action to rebuild it. This could entail expressing genuine regret, discussing avoiding reoccurring problems, and restating the dedication to a reliable procedure.

Building trust among conflict parties in educational settings is delicate and nuanced, but it is essential for achieving lasting and meaningful resolutions. By demonstrating consistency, fostering open communication, promoting transparency, and modeling respect, facilitators can create an environment where trust thrives, paving the way for constructive conflict resolution and stronger relationships within the school community.

CHAPTER 3

RESTORATIVE CONFLICT RESOLUTION PROCESS

Restorative practices in education mark a transformative approach to managing conflicts and building school communities based on principles of empathy, respect, and accountability. Beyond traditional disciplinary methods, restorative practices focus on healing relationships, addressing the underlying causes of behavior, and involving all parties in the resolution process. This introduction explores the foundational concepts of restorative practices in education, highlighting their significance in fostering positive school climates and promoting student growth and learning.

Core Principles of Restorative Practices

At the heart of restorative practices are several core principles aimed at transforming how schools approach conflicts and discipline. These principles emphasize the importance of relationships in the educational process and recognize that behaviors and conflicts are learning opportunities. Key principles include:

- Repairing Harm: Unlike punitive approaches focusing on punishment, restorative practices seek to repair the harm caused by inappropriate behavior. This involves identifying the actions' impact on others and taking steps to make amends.

- Fostering Empathy and Understanding: Restorative practices encourage individuals to empathize with those affected by their actions, fostering a deeper understanding of the consequences of their behavior on others.

- Encouraging Accountability: Students are encouraged to take responsibility for their actions, understand how they have affected others, and be actively involved in finding ways to correct them.
- Inclusive Decision-Making: Restorative practices involve all parties affected by a conflict in the resolution process, ensuring that everyone's voice is heard and considered in determining the outcome.

Implementing Restorative Practices in Schools

Implementing restorative practices in schools requires a shift in mindset from punitive measures to those that restore relationships and community. Critical components of this implementation include:

- Restorative Conversations: Casual or structured dialogues that encourage open and honest communication and allow individuals to express their feelings, perspectives, and needs.
- Restorative Circles: A structured process that brings together those affected by a conflict or issue in a safe, supportive environment to discuss the impact, share feelings, and collaboratively find a resolution.
- Restorative Conferences: More formal meetings that address serious incidents involving not just the direct parties but other community members who have been impacted to repair harm and restore relationships.

Benefits of Restorative Practices

The benefits of implementing restorative practices in educational settings are multifaceted, extending beyond conflict resolution to influence the overall school culture:

- Improved Relationships: Restorative practices contribute to a more positive and supportive school environment by focusing on healing and strengthening relationships.
- Reduced Bullying and Misbehavior: Schools that adopt restorative practices often report decreases in bullying, violence, and other forms of misbehavior as students develop greater empathy and respect for others.
- Enhanced Emotional Intelligence: Students learn valuable skills in emotional regulation, empathy, communication, and problem-solving, which are critical for their academic and personal development.
- Inclusive School Climate: Restorative practices promote inclusivity by valuing all voices, encouraging diverse perspectives, and ensuring everyone feels respected and valued.

Challenges and Considerations

While the benefits of restorative practices are significant, their implementation is challenging. Schools must consider training needs for staff, time and resource allocation, and the need for a cultural shift towards restorative approaches. Additionally, ongoing evaluation and adaptation of restorative practices are necessary to meet the evolving needs of the school community.

Introducing restorative practices in education represents a progressive step toward creating school environments that prioritize healing, learning, and community. By focusing on repairing harm, fostering empathy, and encouraging accountability, restorative practices hold the promise of resolving conflicts and nurturing compassionate, resilient, and socially responsible individuals.

Opening Dialogue and Encouraging Empathy Among Parties

Opening dialogue and encouraging empathy among parties are essential to restorative practices in educational settings. These strategies aim to transform the traditional approach to conflict and discipline into a process that fosters understanding, healing, and growth. Education professionals and facilitators can lay the groundwork for effective outcomes that take into account the needs and emotions of all parties involved by encouraging open communication and cultivating empathy.

Opening Dialogue: Creating a Safe Space for Communication

Opening dialogue begins with creating a safe and supportive environment where all parties feel comfortable sharing their experiences and perspectives. This involves setting clear guidelines for respectful communication and ensuring confidentiality. Educators can facilitate this by:

- Modeling Active Listening: Demonstrating active listening shows parties how to engage with one another's stories and perspectives attentively and respectfully. This sets the tone for mutual respect and understanding.
- Using Neutral Language: Employing neutral language avoids assigning blame and helps keep the focus on behaviors and impacts rather than personal characteristics.
- Encouraging Honest Expression: It is crucial to allow parties to express their feelings and thoughts openly, without fear of judgment or retribution. This may involve

sharing their experiences related to the conflict and how it has affected them personally.

Encouraging Empathy: Understanding the Impact of Actions

Encouraging empathy is about helping individuals understand the impact of their actions on others. This empathetic understanding is critical for moving beyond surface-level resolutions to address a conflict's more profound emotional and relational aspects. Strategies to encourage empathy include:

- Sharing Impact Stories: Encouraging parties to share how the conflict has affected them can help others understand their actions' emotional and practical consequences. These stories can be powerful tools for fostering empathy.
- Perspective-Taking Exercises: Activities that encourage individuals to put themselves in someone else's shoes can help them appreciate different viewpoints and the complexity of emotions involved in the conflict.
- Highlighting Common Ground: Identifying shared values, experiences, or goals can help bridge divides and foster a shared humanity among conflicting parties.

The Role of Facilitators in Nurturing Dialogue and Empathy

When it comes to leading the introductory conversation and fostering empathy, facilitators are essential. This includes:

- Navigating Emotional Terrain: Facilitators must be skilled in managing emotions during discussions, ensuring that the dialogue remains constructive even when parties express anger, frustration, or hurt.
- Balancing Voices: Ensuring all parties have equal opportunities to speak and be heard is vital for a fair and

inclusive process. Facilitators may need to guide the conversation to ensure quieter voices are listened to gently.

- Reinforcing Constructive Engagement: Facilitators should reinforce positive communication practices and empathetic engagement, acknowledging and praising efforts towards understanding and reconciliation throughout the dialogue.

Building towards Resolution

The conflict resolution process becomes a journey towards mutual understanding and healing by opening dialogue and encouraging empathy. This approach addresses the immediate issues at hand and lays the groundwork for stronger relationships and a more cohesive school community. Through these vital conversations, parties can move from conflict towards collaboration, identifying shared solutions that meet the needs of all involved.

Opening dialogue and encouraging empathy are pivotal for effective conflict resolution in educational settings. These strategies go beyond mere problem-solving to address conflicts' underlying emotional and relational dynamics. By fostering open communication and empathetic understanding, educators and facilitators can help transform conflicts into opportunities for growth, learning, and stronger community bonds.

Identifying the Needs and Interests of Involved Parties

Identifying the needs and interests of involved parties is a critical step in the framework of restorative practices within educational settings. This process goes beyond the surface-level aspects of a conflict to explore the underlying motivations, concerns, and desires that may have contributed to the dispute. By understanding these deeper layers, facilitators and educators can tailor the resolution process to address the root causes of conflicts, facilitating more effective and meaningful outcomes.

Understanding Needs and Interests

The needs and interests of involved parties often reflect fundamental human desires for respect, understanding, safety, belonging, and fairness. In a school context, these manifest as a student's need for recognition, a teacher's interest in maintaining classroom order, or a parent's concern for their child's well-being. Recognizing these needs and interests requires:

- Active Listening and Inquiry: Engaging in active listening and asking open-ended questions helps uncover the deeper motivations behind parties' positions. This approach encourages individuals to express what they want and why it matters to them.
- Empathy and Validation: Demonstrating empathy for each party's needs and interests and validating their feelings and concerns fosters a supportive environment. This validation is crucial for making individuals feel understood and respected, laying the groundwork for constructive dialogue.
- Differentiating Needs from Solutions: It's important to distinguish between the conflict's needs and interests and the proposed solutions. By focusing on needs, parties can explore resolutions that satisfy all involved parties.

Techniques for Identifying Needs and Interests

Several techniques can aid in the process of identifying the needs and interests of conflicting parties:

- Conflict Mapping: Creating a visual representation of the conflict, including the parties involved, their perceived

50

needs and interests, and the relationships between these elements, can provide clarity and insight.

- Role Reversal Exercises: Empathy and a more thorough grasp of the dispute from various angles can be fostered by encouraging parties to communicate what they believe to be the needs and interests of the other party.
- Needs and Interests Workshops: Conducting workshops that focus on exploring needs and interests, using tools like the "Five Whys" technique, can help parties drill down to the core of what they genuinely seek from the resolution process.

The Role of Needs and Interests in Crafting Solutions

With a clear understanding of the needs and interests at play, facilitators can guide parties toward collaborative problem-solving. This involves:

- Generating Options: Exploring innovative possibilities that satisfy the requirements and interests of all parties concerned is made possible by encouraging parties to explore a wide range of potential solutions without passing judgment.
- Evaluating Solutions: Assessing proposed solutions based on their ability to satisfy the identified needs and interests helps narrow the options to those most likely to result in a sustainable resolution.
- Building Agreements: Crafting agreements that articulate how the chosen solutions address the needs and interests of all parties ensures clarity and mutual commitment to the resolution.

Fostering a Restorative Culture

Identifying the needs and interests of involved parties is crucial for resolving individual conflicts and fostering a vital culture within schools. Emphasizing empathy and understanding in all interactions, this method promotes a school climate where disagreements are seen as chances for learning and development. By routinely engaging in this process, schools can build a community where students, teachers, and parents feel heard, valued, and connected.

Identifying the needs and interests of involved parties is a foundational aspect of restorative practices in education. This process enables a deeper understanding of conflicts and facilitates the development of respectful, equitable, and lasting resolutions. Educators and facilitators can transform conflicts into catalysts for positive change and more robust community bonds by focusing on the human elements at the heart of disputes.

Generating Options for Mutually Acceptable Resolutions

Generating options for mutually acceptable resolutions is pivotal in the restorative conflict resolution process within educational environments. This phase involves collaborative brainstorming and creative thinking to develop solutions that address the needs and interests of all parties involved. It encourages participants to move beyond their initial positions and consider broader possibilities, fostering a spirit of cooperation and compromise. Successfully generating and selecting these options not only resolves the immediate conflict but also strengthens relationships and builds a foundation for positive interactions in the future.

Collaborative Brainstorming

The process begins with collaborative brainstorming sessions, where all parties are encouraged to contribute ideas without judgment or criticism. This open and inclusive approach ensures that diverse perspectives are considered, enhancing the likelihood of finding innovative and satisfactory solutions. Facilitators are crucial in guiding this process, ensuring the conversation remains focused and constructive.

- Creating a Safe and Creative Space: Creating an environment where people feel free to express their ideas and opinions is critical. This might involve setting ground rules emphasizing respect and confidentiality and suspending judgment during brainstorming.
- Encouraging Creative Thinking: Participants are encouraged to think outside the box and propose various solutions, including those that may initially seem unconventional. The goal is to generate multiple options that can be evaluated and refined later.

Identifying Mutual Gains

A key objective of generating options is identifying solutions that offer mutual gains for all parties involved. This requires participants to look for areas of overlap in their needs and interests, where compromises can lead to shared benefits.

- Focusing on Interests, Not Positions: By concentrating on the underlying interests rather than fixed positions, parties can uncover common ground and explore solutions that offer reciprocal advantages.
- Exploring Different Scenarios: Discussing various scenarios and their potential outcomes can help participants visualize the practical implications of different

options, facilitating a more informed decision-making process.

Evaluating and Refining Options

After various choices have been produced, the following stage assesses each one to ascertain its viability, appeal, and possible effects on every party.

- Criteria-Based Evaluation: Developing criteria based on the identified needs and interests allows for systematically assessing each option. Criteria may include fairness, effectiveness, timeliness, and sustainability.
- Iterative Refinement: Through discussion and negotiation, options can be refined, combined, or modified to better meet the needs of all parties. This iterative process encourages flexibility and creativity in finding the most suitable resolution.

Building Consensus

The ultimate goal of generating options is to build consensus around an acceptable resolution for all parties. This involves:

- Prioritizing Options: Ranking the options based on their evaluation can help focus discussions on the most promising solutions.
- Negotiating Details: Once a preferred option is identified, parties can negotiate the specifics of the agreement, ensuring that all concerns are addressed and expectations are clear.
- Formalizing Agreements: Documenting the agreed-upon resolution and outlining the steps for implementation ensures that all parties are committed to the outcome and understand their responsibilities.

Emphasizing Future Relationships

Throughout the process of generating options for mutually acceptable resolutions, an emphasis is placed on resolving the current conflict and preserving and strengthening relationships for the future. This forward-looking perspective encourages participants to consider the long-term implications of their decisions and to prioritize solutions that contribute to a positive and supportive educational environment.

Generating options for mutually acceptable resolutions is a dynamic and collaborative process at schools' heart of restorative conflict resolution. By engaging all parties in creative problem-solving, focusing on mutual gains, and building consensus, educational communities can resolve conflicts in a way that respects the needs and interests of everyone involved, fostering a culture of understanding, cooperation, and respect.

Evaluating Options Based on Fairness and Equity

Evaluating options based on fairness and equity is critical in educational settings' therapeutic conflict resolution process. This stage ensures that the solutions proposed during the brainstorming phase are assessed through justice and impartiality, addressing the needs and concerns of all parties involved. The emphasis on fairness and equity not only aids in finding a resolution acceptable to everyone but also reinforces the principles of respect and dignity, which are central to restorative practices.

Establishing Criteria for Fairness and Equity

The process begins by establishing clear criteria to guide the options' evaluation. These criteria might include considerations such as:

- Equal Representation: Ensuring that the voices and perspectives of all parties have been considered in the development of solutions.
- Impartiality: Assessing options without bias towards any individual or group.
- Accessibility: Ensuring the resolution is achievable and practical for all parties involved, considering any barriers preventing equitable implementation.
- Impact: Considering the short-term and long-term effects of the resolution on the individuals and the wider school community.

Involving All Parties in the Evaluation Process

Involving all parties in the evaluation process is essential for maintaining transparency and building trust. This collaborative approach allows individuals to express their views on the fairness and equity of each option, contributing to a more comprehensive and inclusive assessment.

- Facilitated Discussions: Organizing discussions where parties can express their opinions on the options, guided by the established criteria for fairness and equity.
- Feedback Mechanisms: Providing avenues for parties to offer feedback anonymously, ensuring that all perspectives are heard without fear of repercussion.

Weighing the Options

With the criteria for fairness and equity in place, parties can weigh the options against these benchmarks. This involves a detailed examination of how each solution meets the principles of justice and impartiality and addresses the needs and rights of all involved.

- Comparative Analysis: Conducting a side-by-side comparison of how each option fares in terms of fairness and equity, considering the parties' diverse needs and perspectives.
- Pros and Cons: Outlining each option's benefits and drawbacks from the perspectives of equality and fairness will help decision-makers make better decisions.

Seeking External Input

In some cases, seeking input from external sources can provide additional insights into the fairness and equity of the proposed options. This might include consulting with other educators, conflict resolution experts, or legal advisors who can offer an objective perspective.

Making Adjustments

Based on the evaluation, adjustments may be necessary to ensure that the selected resolution aligns with the principles of fairness and equity. This iterative process allows for fine-tuning the options to better meet the needs of all parties in a just and equitable manner.

- Modification: Modifying options to address any concerns or imbalances identified during the evaluation process.
- Combination: Combining elements of different options to create a hybrid solution that more fully meets the criteria for fairness and equity.

Reaching Consensus

The ultimate goal of evaluating options based on fairness and equity is to reach a consensus on a resolution that all parties can support. This consensus-building process is facilitated by a shared commitment to finding a solution that respects the dignity and rights of everyone involved.

Evaluating options based on fairness and equity is fundamental to educational environments' therapeutic conflict resolution process. By applying these principles, schools can ensure that the resolutions reached not only solve the immediate conflict but also uphold the values of justice and respect essential for fostering a positive and inclusive community. This careful evaluation reinforces the commitment to treating all parties fairly and ensures that the solutions developed are equitable and sustainable in the long term.

Facilitating Agreement and Implementation of Resolutions

Facilitating agreement and the implementation of resolutions is a vital phase in the therapeutic conflict resolution process within schools. This stage marks the transition from discussion and decision-making to action, requiring careful planning, communication, and follow-through to ensure that the agreed-upon solutions are effectively implemented. Achieving consensus on a resolution represents a collective commitment to move forward, but the actual test of the process lies in the successful implementation of these agreements.

The facilitator, in their pivotal role, acts as a mediator to guide the parties through the finalization of their agreement and oversees the implementation phase. Their guidance ensures that the resolution is clearly articulated, with specific actions, responsibilities, and timelines outlined. This clarity is paramount to avoid misunderstandings and ensure that all parties are aligned with their commitments.

Communication, a powerful tool during this phase, is key. The facilitator must ensure that the agreement is effectively communicated to all relevant stakeholders, including those who may not have been directly involved in the conflict resolution process but who are affected by the outcome. This might include other students, staff members, or even the wider school community, depending on the nature of the conflict. Effective communication helps to build broader support for the resolution and fosters a sense of collective responsibility for maintaining a positive and respectful school environment.

Monitoring the implementation of the resolution is another critical aspect of this phase. The facilitator and designated parties should establish regular check-ins to assess progress, address any challenges that arise, and make adjustments as necessary. These monitoring efforts help maintain momentum and demonstrate a continued commitment to the resolution, reinforcing trust among the parties and the school community.

Flexibility is essential during the implementation phase. Despite the best planning, unforeseen challenges may emerge, necessitating adjustments to the original agreement. A flexible approach allows parties to navigate these challenges without derailing the resolution process. It also underscores the vital principle of addressing human needs and relationships, which are often dynamic and complex.

Lastly, acknowledging accomplishments—no matter how tiny—is a useful tool rather than only a formality. Acknowledging progress and achievements along the way not only motivates continued adherence to the agreement but also reinforces the positive impacts of the restorative conflict resolution process. Celebrations can help to solidify the changes in relationships and behaviors, contributing to a lasting transformation within the school community.

In facilitating agreement and the implementation of resolutions, the emphasis is on action, accountability, and adaptability. By carefully guiding this phase, facilitators can help ensure that the resolutions reached through the therapeutic process are not just theoretical solutions but are actively lived out within the school, leading to genuine healing, growth, and positive change. This phase is a testament to the collective effort of all involved to move beyond conflict, embracing a shared vision for a harmonious and supportive educational environment.

Post-Resolution: Ensuring the Agreement is sustained and Effective

Post-resolution, ensuring the agreement is sustained and effective, marks a crucial phase in restorative conflict resolution, especially in educational settings. This stage focuses on the long-term success of the agreements made, aiming to solidify the positive changes in behavior and relationships and to prevent the recurrence of similar conflicts. The effectiveness of a resolution is not merely in its immediate resolution of the conflict but in its enduring impact on the parties involved and the broader school community.

After reaching an agreement and beginning its implementation, the continuous involvement of facilitators or designated school staff is crucial. Their efforts are required to maintain the momentum and ensure the commitments are honored. This involves regular monitoring and follow-up. These follow-ups act as checkpoints to evaluate if the resolution still meets the needs of all parties involved and how well the agreement conditions are being followed.

An essential component of sustaining the agreement is the availability of support for the parties involved. This support may come in various forms, including counseling, mediation services, or academic assistance, depending on the nature of the initial conflict and the terms of the resolution. Giving people continuous support makes it easier for them to deal with the difficulties of following the agreement and shows how seriously the school takes the welfare of its employees and pupils.

In the post-resolution stage, feedback mechanisms are essential. Encouraging open and honest communication about the effectiveness of the resolution is critical. This allows for identifying any issues or dissatisfaction that may arise post-resolution. Such feedback can inform adjustments to the agreement or the implementation of additional support measures, ensuring that the resolution remains responsive to the evolving needs of the parties involved.

Education on conflict resolution and restorative practices should continue to be a priority. Workshops, training sessions, and curriculum integration focusing on conflict management, communication skills, and emotional intelligence can equip students and staff with the tools they need to constructively and empathetically manage disputes by fostering a school culture that values and practices therapeutic principles, the likelihood of conflicts escalating to the point of needing formal resolution is reduced.

Celebrating successes is as essential in the post-resolution phase as during the resolution process. Recognizing and highlighting the agreement's positive outcomes—such as improved relationships, enhanced communication, or achieving mutual goals—can motivate continued adherence to the agreement and inspire others in the school community to embrace restorative approaches.

Post-resolution efforts are pivotal in ensuring that agreements are effective in the short term and sustained over time. Schools can ensure that vital conflict resolution leads to lasting positive change through regular monitoring, ongoing support, active feedback loops, continued education, and celebrating successes. This phase underscores the commitment to a holistic and sustained approach to conflict resolution, emphasizing growth, learning, and community cohesion.

CHAPTER 4

COMPLEX NEGOTIATION TACTICS

Understanding the basics of integrative bargaining is essential in navigating complex negotiations and conflicts, especially within educational environments. This approach, often contrasted with distributive bargaining, focuses on collaborative problem-solving and seeks outcomes that are beneficial for all parties involved. Integrative bargaining is grounded in the principle that mutual satisfaction can be achieved through open communication, trust-building, and the exploration of underlying needs and interests.

At the core of integrative bargaining is the recognition that conflicts and negotiations are not zero-sum scenarios where one party's gain is necessarily another's loss. This strategy, on the other hand, makes the assumption that solutions that increase the available value can be developed with innovative thinking and a readiness to consider the viewpoint of others, producing a situation where everyone wins. This methodology is particularly relevant in schools, where the interests of students, teachers, parents, and administrators often intersect and where the overarching goal is the well-being and development of the student body.

Implementing integrative bargaining involves several key steps, starting with the identification of each party's interests. Unlike positions, which are often rigid and specific demands, interests are the underlying reasons for these positions. By focusing on interests, parties can uncover common ground and areas where concessions can be made without sacrificing their core needs. For instance, in a dispute over school resources, understanding that both parties are ultimately interested in enhancing student learning can open up avenues for collaboration that were not initially apparent.

Effective communication is another cornerstone of integrative bargaining. This entails not only clearly articulating one's own interests and concerns but also actively listening to and validating the perspectives of others. Such communication fosters an atmosphere of respect and empathy, essential for building the trust that integrative bargaining requires. In educational settings, where stakeholders come from diverse backgrounds and may have different communication styles, being mindful of and accommodating these differences is crucial.

Another aspect of integrative bargaining is the generation of options. Rather than sticking to predetermined solutions, parties are encouraged to brainstorm collectively, thinking creatively about how to meet the various interests at play. This might involve proposing alternative resource allocations, new educational programs, or different ways of structuring the school day. The key is to remain open to innovative solutions that might not have been considered within a more adversarial negotiation framework.

Finally, integrative bargaining emphasizes the importance of objective criteria in decision-making. Rather than basing agreements on power dynamics or subjective preferences, parties agree to rely on independent standards such as fairness, educational best practices, or legal guidelines. This approach helps ensure that the resolution is not only mutually satisfactory but also grounded in principles that transcend the immediate interests of the parties involved.

Understanding and applying the basics of integrative bargaining can transform how conflicts are resolved within educational environments. By focusing on mutual interests, fostering open and respectful communication, creatively exploring solutions, and grounding decisions in objective criteria, educators and administrators can navigate disputes in a way that strengthens relationships and promotes the collective goals of the educational community. This cooperative strategy not only fixes the current problems but lays the groundwork for future interactions that will be fruitful and constructive.

Approaches to Multi-Party Negotiations

Approaches to multi-party negotiations within educational environments require navigating the complexities that arise when multiple stakeholders are involved. These situations often feature diverse interests, perspectives, and priorities, making the negotiation process more challenging and offering unique opportunities for collaborative problem-solving and innovation. Successful multi-party negotiations hinge on strategies that foster cooperation, ensure equitable participation, and aim for solutions that address the collective needs of all parties.

One fundamental approach is establishing clear communication channels. Effective communication is the bedrock of any negotiation process, but it becomes even more critical when multiple parties are involved. Ensuring that each stakeholder has the opportunity to voice their concerns and contributions is crucial. This might involve structured meetings, using facilitators to manage discussions, and implementing tools and technologies that facilitate group communication. Transparent and open dialogue helps prevent misunderstandings and builds trust among the parties.

Creating a shared understanding of the negotiation's objectives can unify disparate groups. Developing a common goal or vision that all parties can rally behind early in the process sets a positive tone for the negotiations. In the context of schools, this might be a commitment to enhancing student welfare, improving educational outcomes, or fostering a more inclusive school culture. A shared objective is a constant reminder of why the negotiation is taking place, helping keep discussions focused and constructive.

Another critical approach involves breaking down the negotiation into manageable parts. Multi-party negotiations can quickly become unwieldy due to the many issues and interests involved. Parties can tackle problems more effectively and make incremental progress by segmenting the negotiation into smaller, more focused discussions. This strategy also allows for more detailed exploration of specific topics, ensuring that all aspects of the talks receive the attention they deserve.

Incorporating principles of fairness and equity is essential in multi-party negotiations. With multiple stakeholders, ensuring that the process and outcomes are perceived as fair by all parties is vital for the long-term success of the agreement. This might involve rotating leadership roles, using neutral facilitators, or establishing rules that guarantee each party equal speaking time. Equitable participation reinforces the validity of the negotiation process and the credibility of the solutions developed.

Building consensus is a central goal of multi-party negotiations. Unlike in dyadic negotiations, where reaching a bilateral agreement might be straightforward, multi-party contexts require finding common ground among a broader range of stakeholders. Techniques such as brainstorming sessions, voting mechanisms, or decision-making matrices can help identify options with broad support. Achieving consensus ensures that the agreement reflects the collective will of the parties and enhances its sustainability.

Finally, planning for implementation and follow-up is crucial. Multi-party agreements often involve complex logistics and the cooperation of various stakeholders for successful implementation. Establishing clear action plans, responsibilities, and timelines during the negotiation ensures everyone is on the same page. Additionally, setting regular check-ins and review meetings post-agreement can help address any issues during implementation and adjust plans as necessary.

Approaches to multi-party negotiations in educational settings must navigate the added complexity of diverse stakeholder groups. Strategies that emphasize clear communication, shared objectives, manageable discussion segments, fairness, consensus-building, and careful implementation planning can lead to successful outcomes. These approaches resolve the immediate issues and contribute to building more robust, collaborative educational communities.

The Role of Mediation and Facilitation in Conflict Resolution

Mediation and facilitation in conflict resolution within educational settings are pivotal in navigating disputes and fostering a constructive dialogue among parties. These processes are integral to restorative practices, emphasizing the importance of communication, understanding, and collaborative problem-solving. Mediators and facilitators bring a neutral perspective to conflicts, guiding discussions in a way that encourages mutual respect and empathy and, ultimately, leads to resolutions that reflect the collective interests and needs of those involved.

The disputing parties can work with a mediator or a neutral third party to find a solution that works for both of them. In educational contexts, mediators often deal with disputes between students, staff members, or students and staff. The mediator's role is not to decide the outcome but to facilitate communication, help clarify the issues, and explore potential solutions. This process empowers the parties to take control of the resolution, ensuring that the outcome is tailored to their specific circumstances and needs. Mediation is particularly effective in educational settings because it respects the parties' autonomy and emphasizes restoring relationships rather than imposing punitive measures.

Facilitation, while similar to mediation, often involves guiding a group through a structured process to achieve a specific objective, such as developing a shared vision, planning a project, or resolving a complex issue involving multiple stakeholders. Facilitators manage the discussion to ensure it is productive, inclusive and focused on the goal. Facilitation can be crucial in schools during staff meetings, parent-teacher associations, or student council discussions, where diverse viewpoints and interests must be harmonized to reach a consensus or make collective decisions.

Both mediation and facilitation rely heavily on a set of core skills and principles:

- Active Listening: Encouraging all parties to listen to each other's perspectives without interruption fosters a deeper understanding of the underlying issues and concerns.
- Empathy: Promoting an empathetic approach helps participants see the conflict from the other party's viewpoint, often revealing common ground and facilitating compromise.
- Neutrality: Maintaining neutrality ensures that the mediator or facilitator is perceived as unbiased, which is essential for building trust.
- Confidentiality: Keeping the discussions confidential encourages open and honest communication, as parties feel safe to express their thoughts and feelings.
- Problem-Solving: Guiding the parties through a structured problem-solving process helps identify creative and mutually satisfactory solutions.

Effective mediation and facilitation can transform educational environments. By resolving conflicts in a way that addresses the root causes and repairs relationships, schools can create a more positive and supportive atmosphere conducive to learning. Furthermore, these processes model valuable life skills for students, including communication, empathy, negotiation, and cooperation, which are essential for their personal and professional development.

Mediation and facilitation in educational conflict resolution are crucial for not only resolving disputes but also building stronger, more cohesive school communities. These approaches encourage a shift away from adversarial methods towards more collaborative, restorative practices, reflecting a commitment to understanding, respect, and mutual growth among all members of the educational community.

Using Data and Evidence to Support Negotiation Claims

Using data and evidence to support negotiation claims enhances the credibility and effectiveness of the negotiation process, especially in educational settings. This approach involves gathering relevant information, statistics, research findings, and case studies to support positions and proposals, ensuring that discussions are grounded in reality, not just personal opinions or emotions. By relying on objective data, negotiators can construct more persuasive arguments, identify areas of common interest, and facilitate the resolution of disputes rationally and equitably.

In the educational sector, where decisions can significantly impact student outcomes, staff well-being, and institutional integrity, the importance of data-driven negotiation cannot be overstated. Evidence provides a solid foundation for constructive dialogue when negotiating resource allocations, policy changes, or conflict resolutions. For instance, when discussing the need for smaller class sizes, presenting data on student-teacher ratios and their impact on learning outcomes can be a compelling argument that is difficult to ignore.

Data and evidence also play a critical role in overcoming biases and preconceptions. In complex negotiations involving multiple parties, it's easy for discussions to become mired in subjective viewpoints. Objective data acts as a neutral arbiter, helping to refocus the conversation on factual bases and shared goals. This is particularly valuable in educational settings, where the stakes are high, and decisions affect diverse stakeholder groups with varying interests and perspectives.

Moreover, using data and evidence encourages transparency and accountability in the negotiation process. When parties come to the table armed with verifiable information, it sets a tone of openness and honesty. It also provides a clear rationale for proposed solutions, making it easier for all involved to understand the reasoning behind certain positions and to evaluate the merits of different options objectively.

However, for data and evidence to be effective in supporting negotiation claims, it must be relevant, accurate, and current. This requires thorough preparation, including researching the issue, collecting data from reliable sources, and analyzing the information to understand its implications. Additionally, negotiators must be adept at presenting data in a clear and accessible manner, using visuals or summaries to highlight key points and ensure that the evidence is understandable to all parties, regardless of their background or expertise.

In some cases, negotiators may need to collaborate to identify mutually agreed-upon data sources or to commission joint research. This collaborative approach to information gathering can further enhance trust and cooperation among parties, laying a stronger foundation for reaching a consensus.

Ultimately, using data and evidence to support negotiation claims is about more than just strengthening one's position; it's about fostering a more informed, respectful, and productive negotiation process. In educational settings, where the outcomes of negotiations can have far-reaching consequences, the value of a data-driven approach is immeasurable. It ensures that decisions are made based on the best available evidence, leading to outcomes that are not only fair and equitable but also in the best interest of the educational community.

Managing Power Dynamics and Imbalances During Negotiation

Managing power dynamics and imbalances during negotiation is crucial, especially in educational environments where stakeholders have varying degrees of influence and authority. Negotiations can quickly become unproductive or unfair if these power imbalances are not acknowledged and addressed. Ensuring everyone has an equal opportunity to participate and express their thoughts is essential to achieving equitable and long-lasting outcomes.

Different positions (e.g., administrators vs. instructors, teachers vs. students), access to resources, knowledge, or even the degree of community support can all contribute to power imbalances in educational contexts. These imbalances affect the negotiation process, with those in more powerful positions dominating discussions while those with less power may feel their needs and perspectives are being overlooked.

To manage these dynamics effectively, it's essential to establish a negotiation framework that levels the playing field. This can involve setting clear ground rules, prioritizing respectful dialogue, equal speaking time, and considering all viewpoints. Such rules not only help to mitigate the influence of power imbalances but also foster a more collaborative atmosphere.

Utilizing a neutral facilitator can also be pivotal in managing power dynamics. A skilled facilitator can ensure that the negotiation process remains balanced, guiding the discussion to allow for equal participation. They can also intervene to prevent any party from overpowering the conversation, ensuring that the negotiation focuses on achieving mutually beneficial outcomes.

Creating opportunities for private discussions or caucuses can also be beneficial. These private meetings allow less powerful parties to discuss their positions and strategies without feeling pressured or overshadowed by more dominant participants. This can help level the negotiation field, allowing all parties to articulate their needs and concerns more confidently.

Another effective strategy is to focus on interests rather than positions. By encouraging parties to explore the underlying reasons behind their demands, the negotiation can shift from a competition for resources or wins to a collaborative problem-solving process. This approach diminishes the impact of power imbalances by concentrating on common goals and shared benefits rather than on who has more influence or control.

Educating all parties about the negotiation process and the issues at stake can also reduce power imbalances. When well-informed, participants are better equipped to confidently and effectively engage in the negotiation. Access to relevant data, research findings, and background information can empower less dominant parties, making the negotiation more equitable.

Finally, establishing a follow-up mechanism is essential to ensure that agreements are implemented relatively and address any persistent power imbalances. Regular check-ins and assessments can help identify whether the agreement's terms are being met and whether any adjustments are needed to account for changes in the power dynamics.

Managing power dynamics and imbalances during negotiation is essential for ensuring that the process is fair, respectful, and productive. By implementing strategies that promote equality, transparency, and collaboration, educational institutions can navigate negotiations in a way that honors the contributions and needs of all stakeholders. Encouraging a climate of respect and understanding among all members of the community not only results in more lasting and successful resolutions but also strengthens it as a whole.

Techniques for Ensuring Balanced Negotiation Outcomes

Techniques for ensuring balanced negotiation outcomes are vital in educational settings that foster an environment of equity and mutual respect among diverse stakeholders. Achieving a balance in negotiation outcomes ensures that all parties feel their concerns have been addressed and their needs met, fostering long-term cooperation and harmony within the school community. This balanced approach to negotiation is critical in education, where the well-being and development of students are paramount.

One key technique is to clearly define the negotiation's objectives from the outset. Having a shared understanding of what the negotiation seeks to achieve can guide the process and help ensure that outcomes align with the educational institution's collective goals. This clarity prevents the negotiation from becoming sidetracked by individual interests and keeps the focus on achieving results that benefit the entire school community.

Active listening is another critical technique. By genuinely listening to and understanding the perspectives and needs of all parties, negotiators can identify common ground and areas where compromise is possible. Active listening also signals respect for each participant's viewpoint, facilitating a more collaborative negotiation atmosphere and leading to more balanced outcomes.

Using objective criteria in decision-making is a powerful tool for ensuring balanced outcomes. Instead of relying on subjective opinions or the influence of power dynamics, negotiations can be guided by data, best practices, and educational standards. This approach lends credibility to the negotiation process and helps ensure that outcomes are fair and rooted in the best interests of the academic community.

Encouraging creative problem-solving is essential for achieving balanced negotiation outcomes. When parties are invited to think creatively and propose innovative solutions, the negotiation can uncover options that might not have been considered initially. This openness to creativity can lead to win-win outcomes that address the needs of all parties in ways that traditional negotiation tactics might not achieve.

Establishing a culture of empathy within the negotiation process can also contribute to balanced outcomes. When negotiators make a concerted effort to understand the emotions and motivations behind each party's position, it fosters a sense of mutual respect and care. This empathetic approach can break down barriers and facilitate agreements that consider the well-being of all stakeholders.

Another technique involves setting up mechanisms for follow-up and evaluation post-negotiation. Ensuring that the agreed-upon outcomes are implemented as planned and evaluating their impact over time can help maintain the balance achieved during the negotiation. This ongoing assessment allows for adjustments as necessary, ensuring that the outcomes continue to meet the needs of all parties.

Finally, providing negotiation training and resources to all stakeholders can empower participants and level the playing field, mainly when power imbalances exist. When everyone has access to negotiation skills and strategies training, it enhances all parties' capacity to engage effectively in the negotiation process, contributing to more balanced outcomes.

Achieving balanced negotiation outcomes in educational settings requires a multifaceted approach that values clarity, active listening, objectivity, creativity, empathy, and ongoing assessment. By employing these techniques, academic institutions can navigate negotiations in a way that not only resolves immediate issues but also strengthens the community, ensuring that decisions are made with the collective well-being and future of the school in mind.

Case Studies on Successful Negotiation in Educational Settings

Studies of successful negotiations in educational contexts offer insightful information on the tactics and methods that can result in constructive outcomes and efficient dispute resolution. These real-world examples illustrate how schools and educational institutions navigate complex negotiations, achieving solutions that benefit all parties involved. Through analyzing these case studies, educators, administrators, and policymakers can better understand the principles of effective negotiation and how they can be applied in various educational contexts.

Case Study 1: Resource Allocation Negotiation

In a large urban school district facing budget cuts, administrators, teachers, and parents have successfully negotiated the redistribution of resources to prioritize student learning and teacher support. The negotiation focused on maintaining essential programs, minimizing layoffs, and identifying alternative funding sources. Through facilitated discussions, stakeholders agreed on a plan that included reallocating funds from non-essential projects, increasing community fundraising efforts, and applying for grants. The outcome was a balanced budget that preserved vital educational programs and minimized the impact on staff and students.

Key Strategies

- Establishing a shared goal of minimizing the impact of budget cuts on student learning.
- Utilizing data and evidence to inform decision-making.
- Engaging in creative problem-solving to identify alternative funding sources.

Case Study 2: Curriculum Development Dispute

A dispute arose in a suburban high school over proposed changes to the history curriculum, with teachers advocating for a more inclusive approach and parents expressing concerns about removing traditional content. Workshops and open forums were organized to facilitate dialogue between teachers, parents, and students. By openly discussing the goals of the curriculum revision and exploring various perspectives, the parties reached a consensus on a curriculum incorporating diverse viewpoints while maintaining core historical knowledge. The process strengthened the school community's cohesion and demonstrated the value of inclusive dialogue in educational decision-making.

Key Strategies

- Creating open channels for communication and feedback.
- Focusing on educational goals and the benefits of a diverse curriculum.
- Building consensus through inclusive and participatory processes.

Case Study 3: Teacher Contract Negotiations

In a rural school district, teacher contract negotiations had reached a stalemate, with teachers seeking better pay and smaller class sizes and the district citing budget constraints. A neutral facilitator was brought in to mediate the negotiations, helping both sides articulate their interests and explore potential compromises. The eventual agreement included:

- A modest salary increase.
- Phased reductions in class sizes.
- A commitment to seek additional funding for the following school year.

The negotiation process fostered a better understanding between teachers and the administration, setting a positive tone for future collaboration.

Key Strategies:

- A neutral facilitator will be employed to guide discussions.
- Identifying mutual interests and areas for compromise.
- Committing to ongoing dialogue and problem-solving.

The aforementioned case examples underscore the significance of effective communication, empathy, and innovative problem-solving techniques in the context of educational negotiating processes. Schools can navigate conflicts and challenges by focusing on shared goals, engaging all stakeholders, and employing effective negotiation strategies, resulting in outcomes that enhance the educational environment for all.

CHAPTER 5

ENSURING BALANCED OUTCOMES

Addressing participants' emotional and psychological needs is crucial in ensuring balanced outcomes in conflict resolution within educational settings. This aspect of the resolution process acknowledges that conflicts are not just about differing opinions or interests but also about the feelings, emotions, and psychological well-being of those involved. The role of facilitators and educators is pivotal in creating a more compassionate and supportive environment that fosters genuine understanding and reconciliation by paying attention to these emotional and psychological dimensions.

Conflicts, by their very nature, can elicit strong emotional responses, including frustration, anger, disappointment, and hurt. If not acknowledged and managed sensitively, these emotions can hinder the resolution process and lead to further misunderstandings or resentment. Therefore, it is essential to create a space where participants feel safe to express their emotions and feel assured that their emotional experiences are valid and respected. This emotional acknowledgment can pave the way for more effective communication and collaborative problem-solving.

One approach to addressing these needs is active listening, a crucial practice where the facilitator or mediator pays close attention to what is being said and the underlying emotions. This practice helps understand the root causes of the conflict and demonstrates empathy and validation, which are critical ingredients in building trust and openness among participants. Recognizing and naming the emotions involved can also help de-escalate tensions and make participants feel seen and heard, a critical step towards healing and resolution.

Moreover, integrating techniques focusing on emotional regulation and stress management into the resolution process can be beneficial. Strategies like mindfulness exercises, quick guided relaxations, or just providing breaks throughout conversations for participants to gather their thoughts and control their emotions enhance the general tone of the negotiation. These practices acknowledge the human aspect of conflicts and help maintain a constructive and respectful dialogue.

Understanding the psychological impact of conflicts is also paramount. Long-standing or particularly acrimonious disputes can leave individuals feeling vulnerable, anxious, or even traumatized. To address these psychological needs, it may be necessary to give people who require access to therapy or support groups. In educational settings, where students and staff should feel safe and supported, ensuring psychological well-being is as important as resolving the immediate conflict.

Additionally, training educators, administrators, and even students in essential emotional intelligence and conflict resolution skills is a significant step that can equip them with the tools needed to navigate disputes more effectively in the future. Such training can foster a culture of empathy, resilience, and mutual respect within the school community, reducing the likelihood of conflicts escalating and improving the overall school climate.

Addressing participants' emotional and psychological needs is integral to achieving balanced conflict resolution outcomes in educational settings. By acknowledging and managing the emotional dimensions of conflicts, facilitators can guide the negotiation process toward more compassionate and constructive resolutions. This approach addresses the immediate issues, promotes healing, and strengthens relationships, contributing to a more supportive and harmonious educational environment.

Fostering Accountability and Responsibility Post-Conflict

Fostering accountability and responsibility post-conflict is critical to ensuring that the resolutions reached during the conflict resolution process are implemented and contribute to personal growth and the strengthening of the school community. This approach underscores the importance of individuals taking ownership of their actions, understanding the impact of these actions on others, and committing to positive changes that prevent future conflicts. In educational settings, where learning and development are paramount, fostering accountability and responsibility helps instill essential life skills in students while enhancing the overall climate of trust and mutual respect.

Achieving accountability involves explicitly acknowledging the behaviors or actions contributing to the conflict. This acknowledgment is crucial for moving forward, as it validates the experiences and feelings of those affected by the conflict. However, this process must be framed positively, focusing on learning and improvement rather than punishment or blame. In doing so, individuals are encouraged to reflect on their actions, consider how they can make amends, and contribute to healing any harm caused.

Responsibility, on the other hand, extends beyond acknowledgment. It involves taking concrete steps to address the consequences of one's actions and making commitments to change behavior in the future. In a school setting, this might involve personal apologies, participation in restorative practices such as community service or peer mediation programs, or engagement in workshops on conflict resolution and empathy building. These actions not only help repair relationships but also demonstrate a genuine commitment to personal growth and the well-being of the school community.

Facilitators and educators play a crucial role in guiding individuals through this process, offering support and resources that enable them to fulfill their responsibilities. This might include setting up structured follow-up meetings to check progress, providing access to counseling or mentorship programs, or involving them in initiatives promoting a positive school culture. By actively supporting individuals in taking responsibility, schools reinforce the message that accountability is valued and essential for community cohesion.

Moreover, fostering a culture of accountability and responsibility within the school requires clear communication of expectations and norms regarding behavior and conflict resolution. This involves addressing conflicts as they arise and proactively teaching and modeling values such as empathy, respect, and integrity. Integrating these values into the curriculum, school policies, and everyday interactions helps create an environment where students and staff are more likely to take responsibility for their actions and work towards constructive solutions.

Additionally, celebrating successes and recognizing individuals who demonstrate accountability and responsibility can reinforce these behaviors and inspire others. Acknowledgments, whether through formal recognition programs or simple acts of appreciation, highlight the positive impact of taking responsibility and encourage a school-wide culture of accountability.

Fostering accountability and responsibility post-conflict is essential for the resolution process to have a lasting and positive impact. By encouraging individuals to acknowledge their actions, take steps to make amends, and commit to positive change, educational settings can not only resolve conflicts more effectively but also promote personal development and a stronger, more cohesive community. This approach aligns with the broader academic mission of preparing students to be responsible, empathetic, and engaged citizens.

The Principles of Restorative Justice in Achieving Balance

The principles of restorative justice, which aim to achieve balance, play a transformative role in conflict resolution within educational settings. They emphasize healing, community cohesion, and equitable outcomes. Unlike traditional punitive approaches, restorative justice focuses on the needs of all involved, including the harmed party, the individual responsible for the harm, and the broader community. This approach seeks to restore balance by addressing the root causes of conflict, repairing relationships, and integrating solutions that contribute to the well-being of the entire school community.

A fundamental principle of restorative justice is the emphasis on repairing harm. This goes beyond mere punishment or disciplinary action to understand the impact of the conflict and actively involve the responsible party in making amends. Whether through reparations, community service, or apology, the objective is to admit the wrongs done and move toward healing. This repair focus helps restore trust and relationships, which is crucial for a balanced and harmonious educational environment.

Another critical principle is the active involvement of all parties in the resolution process. Restorative justice encourages open dialogue and participation, allowing those affected by the conflict to express their feelings, share their perspectives, and contribute to finding a resolution. This inclusive approach ensures that the solutions are more comprehensive and meaningful and empowers individuals to take ownership of the resolution process. Restorative justice encourages justice and respect for one another, which are fundamental balance elements, by providing a voice to all parties.

Restorative justice also prioritizes the reintegration of the responsible party back into the community. Recognizing that exclusion and isolation can exacerbate negative behaviors, this approach seeks to support individuals in making positive changes and offer opportunities for redemption. In educational environments that uphold this idea, students are encouraged to grow from their mistakes rather than letting them define them. This fosters a culture of compassion and support.

The emphasis on community involvement and support is another cornerstone of restorative justice. Conflicts are seen not just as individual issues but as communal concerns that require collective solutions. By engaging the wider school community in the resolution process; restorative justice builds a shared commitment to upholding values such as empathy, responsibility, and respect. This collective approach not only aids in resolving the immediate conflict but also strengthens the school's social fabric, making it more resilient to future challenges.

Finally, restorative justice promotes ongoing dialogue and reflection to achieve balance. This involves regular check-ins with those involved, evaluations of the effectiveness of the resolution, and adjustments as needed. It also includes educational efforts to raise awareness about restorative practices and to build skills in conflict resolution and emotional intelligence. Through continuous learning and adaptation, schools can cultivate an environment where conflicts are addressed in a healing, constructive, and balanced way.

Therapeutic justice principles offer a holistic and humane approach to conflict resolution in educational settings. By focusing on repairing harm, involving all parties, supporting reintegration, engaging the community, and fostering ongoing dialogue, restorative justice achieves balance in a way that nurtures individual growth and community cohesion. This approach resolves conflicts more effectively and creates a more positive, supportive, and equitable educational environment.

Maintaining Confidentiality and Trust Throughout the Process

Maintaining confidentiality and trust throughout the conflict resolution process is paramount in educational settings, where the stakes involve the immediate resolution of disputes and the long-term well-being and cohesion of the school community. This principle is crucial for creating a safe environment where all parties feel respected and secure enough to express their views openly. Confidentiality ensures that sensitive information shared during the process is protected, fostering a climate of trust conducive to honest dialogue and meaningful resolution. On the other hand, trust is the foundation upon which the legitimacy and effectiveness of the conflict resolution process rests. Confidentiality and trust enable a fair, respectful, and transformative process for individuals and the school community.

The Importance of Confidentiality

Confidentiality in conflict resolution involves a commitment to protect the privacy of the information disclosed during the process. In educational environments, this could range from personal feelings and experiences to details about family life or academic performance. The assurance of confidentiality encourages participants to share openly, which is essential for uncovering the root causes of conflicts and for finding solutions that address the needs of all involved. Moreover, respecting confidentiality signals respect for individual dignity and autonomy, which are critical values in educational settings that aim to model ethical behavior for students.

However, maintaining confidentiality is not without challenges. It requires clear guidelines about what information can be shared and with whom, as well as mechanisms for safeguarding it throughout the process. This might involve agreements signed at the outset of the process, secure handling and storage of any documentation, and training for staff and students involved in conflict resolution roles. Navigating these challenges demands a careful balance between protecting privacy and ensuring the process remains transparent and accountable to the broader school community.

Building and Sustaining Trust

Trust in the conflict resolution process is built on fairness, integrity, and impartiality. It is cultivated when participants see the process conducted openly, without bias, and with a genuine commitment to achieving just outcomes. Trust is also reinforced by the competence and empathy of those facilitating the process, whether mediators, teachers, or administrators. Their ability to manage the process effectively, to listen without judgment, and to guide discussions toward constructive solutions plays a crucial role in sustaining participants' faith in the process.

Moreover, trust extends beyond the immediate parties involved in the conflict to the broader school community. Handling conflicts sends a powerful message about the institution's values and culture. A transparent process that consistently respects confidentiality and prioritizes the well-being of participants reinforces trust in the institution's commitment to justice and fairness. Conversely, breaches of privacy or perceived injustices can erode trust, not just in the conflict resolution process but also in the institution.

Strategies for Maintaining Confidentiality and Trust

To effectively maintain confidentiality and trust, educational institutions can employ several strategies. First, establishing clear protocols for the conflict resolution process, including explicit confidentiality agreements, helps set expectations and boundaries. These protocols should be communicated to all participants and reinforced throughout the process.

Training for staff and students involved in conflict resolution roles is essential for equipping them with the skills to handle sensitive information appropriately and navigate conflicts' emotional complexities. This training should emphasize the ethical dimensions of confidentiality and the role of trust in achieving positive outcomes.

Creating a supportive environment that encourages empathy and understanding among all school community members can reinforce trust. This might involve regular discussions about the value of confidentiality, workshops on effective communication and empathy, and opportunities for community building that foster a sense of belonging and mutual respect.

The dispute resolution process can be continuously evaluated through regular review and feedback processes, guaranteeing that it will continue to be efficient and sensitive to community requirements. These include surveys, feedback forms, or debriefing sessions that provide insights into how confidentiality and trust are being maintained and where improvements are needed.

The Impact of Confidentiality and Trust

The impact of effectively maintaining confidentiality and trust is profound. It improves the efficiency of the dispute resolution procedure and supports the development of a supportive school climate marked by justice-seeking, empathy, and respect. Students learn valuable life skills related to communication, ethical behavior, and emotional intelligence, essential for personal and professional development.

Moreover, a school community that successfully navigates conflicts in a manner that respects confidentiality and builds trust is better positioned to face future challenges. The resilience and cohesion fostered through such a process are invaluable assets for any educational institution, contributing to a safer, more supportive, and more vibrant learning environment.

Maintaining confidentiality and trust throughout the conflict resolution process is essential for achieving fair, equitable, healing, and transformative outcomes. By prioritizing these principles, educational settings can navigate the complexities of conflicts with integrity and compassion, laying the foundation for a stronger, more united school community.

Strategies for Preventing the Recurrence of Similar Conflicts

Strategies for preventing the recurrence of similar conflicts in educational settings focus on addressing the root causes of disputes and fostering a culture of open communication, mutual respect, and proactive problem-solving. The goal is to resolve the present conflict and implement practices and policies that reduce the likelihood of similar issues arising. By doing so, educational institutions can create a more harmonious, supportive, and conducive environment for learning and development.

Developing Comprehensive Conflict Resolution Policies

The foundation for preventing future conflicts lies in developing comprehensive conflict resolution policies that are communicated to all school community members. These policies specify how disputes are to be reported and handled, the obligations of all parties participating in the dispute resolution process, and the tools available to assist disputing parties. By having clear, accessible policies, schools demonstrate a commitment to constructively and equitably managing disputes.

Implementing Restorative Practices

Restorative practices offer a holistic approach to conflict resolution that focuses on healing relationships and restoring community cohesion. By integrating restorative practices into the school culture, educational institutions can encourage a shift away from punitive responses to conflicts towards more empathetic and constructive solutions. This might involve restorative circles, peer mediation programs, and training for students and staff in restorative techniques. Such practices not only address the immediate conflict but also work to build stronger, more resilient relationships that can withstand future challenges.

Promoting Emotional Intelligence and Communication Skills

Enhancing the emotional intelligence and communication skills of students and staff is critical to preventing the recurrence of conflicts. Workshops, curricular integration, and focused training programs can help achieve this. Teaching individuals how to express their emotions constructively, listen actively, and engage in empathetic dialogue equips them with the tools to navigate disagreements more effectively and to find common ground with others.

Fostering an Inclusive School Culture

An inclusive school culture that values diversity and promotes equity can significantly reduce the incidence of conflicts. This involves proactive efforts to ensure that all students and staff feel valued, respected, and understood, regardless of their background or identity. Celebrating diversity, addressing bias and discrimination, and creating spaces where diverse perspectives are welcomed and heard can strengthen the sense of community and minimize the triggers for conflict.

Engaging Parents and the Wider Community

It is essential to involve parents and the larger community to resolve and avert future conflicts. Parents can offer valuable insights into their children's behavior and needs, while community resources can provide additional support and interventions. By building strong partnerships with parents and community organizations, schools can create a supportive network contributing to a positive and peaceful educational environment.

Regular Review and Adaptation

Preventing conflict recurrence requires ongoing review and adaptation of policies, practices, and the school culture. This involves regularly assessing the effectiveness of conflict resolution efforts, soliciting feedback from students, staff, and parents, and being open to making changes based on what is learned. Continuous improvement ensures that the school remains responsive to the evolving needs of its community and is better prepared to address future challenges.

Preventing the recurrence of similar conflicts in educational settings demands a comprehensive and proactive approach. Schools can significantly reduce the likelihood of future disputes by developing clear policies, implementing restorative practices, enhancing communication and emotional intelligence, fostering an inclusive culture, engaging the wider community, and committing to regular review and adaptation. These strategies contribute to a more peaceful and supportive learning environment and model essential values and skills students can carry beyond the school gates.

Measuring and Evaluating the Impact of Conflict Resolution

Measuring and evaluating the impact of conflict resolution within educational settings is essential for understanding the effectiveness of the strategies and practices employed. This process assesses whether conflicts have been resolved satisfactorily and gauges the long-term effects on the school community's health and cohesion. Practical evaluation can illuminate areas of success and identify opportunities for improvement, guiding future efforts toward more impactful conflict resolution approaches.

Establishing Clear Evaluation Criteria

The first step in measuring the impact of conflict resolution efforts is to establish clear criteria against which success can be assessed. These criteria include the resolution's immediacy, the parties' satisfaction levels, its durability over time, and its broader impact on the school community's atmosphere and relationships. Setting these benchmarks at the outset ensures that evaluations are focused, objective, and aligned with the goals of the conflict resolution process.

Collecting Diverse Forms of Data

Data from multiple sources must be gathered to get a complete picture of the impact. This might include surveys and feedback forms from the participants directly involved in the conflict and resolution process, interviews or focus groups with broader groups of students and staff to gauge the wider community's perceptions, and quantitative data such as records of recurring conflicts or disciplinary actions. Collecting diverse forms of data ensures a multi-faceted understanding of the conflict resolution process's effectiveness.

Utilizing Feedback Mechanisms

Regular feedback mechanisms are vital for ongoing evaluation. These can be post-resolution surveys, suggestion boxes, or regular check-ins with individuals involved in conflicts. Feedback techniques support an environment of open communication and ongoing development in the school and offer helpful information for assessing the effectiveness of conflict resolution initiatives.

Analyzing Long-term Trends

Evaluating the impact of conflict resolution extends beyond immediate outcomes to include long-term trends. This involves tracking the recurrence of similar conflicts, changes in the school's disciplinary actions, and shifts in the school climate over time. Analyzing these trends can help schools understand the lasting effects of their conflict resolution strategies and identify persistent challenges that require further attention.

Engaging in Reflective Practice

Reflective practice is a powerful tool for evaluation, involving a critical analysis of the conflict resolution process and outcomes. Facilitators, mediators, and school leaders should regularly reflect on their experiences, discussing what worked well, what challenges were encountered, and how the process could be improved. This reflective practice can lead to valuable insights and innovations in conflict resolution strategies.

Reporting and Sharing Findings

Evaluation findings should be reported and shared with the broader school community, including students, staff, and parents. Transparency about conflict resolution efforts' successes and challenges builds trust and encourages community-wide engagement in creating a more peaceful and supportive educational environment.

Committing to Continuous Improvement

Finally, measuring and evaluating the impact of conflict resolution is part of a commitment to continuous improvement. The insights gained from evaluations should inform the development and refinement of conflict resolution policies, practices, and training programs. This commitment to learning and adaptation is crucial for ensuring that conflict resolution efforts remain effective, responsive to the school community's needs, and aligned with education goals.

Measuring and evaluating the impact of conflict resolution is critical to developing effective, sustainable conflict resolution practices in educational settings. Through careful planning, diverse data collection, reflective practice, and a commitment to continuous improvement, schools can enhance their ability to resolve conflicts constructively, contributing to a healthier, more harmonious educational environment.

Long-term Follow-up and Support for Conflict Parties

Long-term follow-up and support for conflict parties are integral to a holistic conflict resolution process within educational settings. This approach recognizes that resolving the immediate dispute is the first step toward healing and rebuilding relationships. Ongoing assistance and consistent follow-up guarantee that the resolutions are carried out and enhance the general well-being of the school community and the personal development of those engaged. By investing in long-term care, educational institutions underscore their commitment to nurturing a supportive, empathetic, and cohesive environment.

Structured Follow-Up Meetings

One effective method for long-term follow-up is through structured meetings scheduled after the resolution has been reached. These meetings offer an opportunity to check in on the progress of the agreed-upon actions, discuss any challenges that have arisen, and adjust plans as necessary. For students, these check-ins can be facilitated by counselors, teachers, or peer mediators involved in the resolution process. For staff conflicts, administrators or human resources personnel might take the lead. The key is to ensure that these follow-ups are conducted in a supportive, non-judgmental atmosphere that encourages honest communication.

Ongoing Emotional and Psychological Support

Conflicts can leave emotional and psychological scars that persist even after resolving the dispute. Providing ongoing support through counseling services, peer support groups, or mentorship programs can help individuals process their experiences, develop coping strategies, and rebuild their well-being. This support is particularly crucial for those who have experienced bullying, discrimination, or other forms of harm that can have lasting impacts on their mental health and academic performance.

Educational Workshops and Training

Continued education on conflict resolution, communication skills, and emotional intelligence can further support the long-term success of conflict parties. Workshops and training sessions in these areas equip individuals with the tools to manage future disagreements more effectively and contribute to a school culture that values understanding, empathy, and cooperation. These educational opportunities should be made available to all school community members, reinforcing that everyone plays a role in creating a harmonious educational environment.

Restorative Practices

Incorporating restorative practices into the follow-up and support phase can aid in the continued healing of relationships and restoring community bonds. Activities such as restorative circles or community service projects can provide platforms for individuals to reflect on their actions, make amends, and contribute positively to the school community. These practices emphasize the importance of reintegration and redemption, offering a path forward for those who have caused harm.

Peer Support Networks

Peer support networks can offer valuable social and emotional support to individuals involved in conflicts. By connecting with peers who have gone through similar experiences, individuals can find understanding, advice, and encouragement. These networks can be facilitated through formal programs or informal arrangements, but the key is creating a sense of belonging and mutual care among participants.

Monitoring and Adjusting Policies and Practices

Long-term follow-up also involves monitoring the effectiveness of school conflict resolution policies and practices. By tracking conflicts and resolution trends, schools can identify areas where adjustments may be needed, whether in response to emerging challenges or as part of continuous improvement efforts. Involving diverse stakeholders in the assessment process, such as parents, staff, and students, guarantees that policies and procedures remain applicable and sensitive to the community's requirements.

Long-term follow-up and support for conflict parties are essential for ensuring the enduring success of conflict resolution efforts in educational settings. Schools can resolve immediate disputes and foster an environment of growth, healing, and unity by providing structured follow-ups, ongoing support, educational opportunities, restorative practices, peer networks, and continuously evaluating and adjusting policies. By taking a comprehensive approach, the educational institution demonstrates its dedication to the welfare of staff and students, establishing the foundation for a productive and good school climate.

CHAPTER 6

POST-CONFLICT RESOLUTION STRATEGIES

Monitoring the implementation of agreements is a crucial step in conflict resolution, particularly within educational settings. This process ensures that the commitments made during negotiations are carried out effectively, fostering trust among all parties involved and reinforcing the integrity of the resolution process. Effective monitoring not only confirms compliance with the agreed-upon terms but also provides an opportunity to address any challenges or adjustments needed, ensuring that the resolution remains relevant and beneficial over time.

The foundation of successful monitoring lies in the clarity and specificity of the agreement itself. Agreements should outline not only each party's responsibilities but also the timelines for implementation and the indicators of success. This level of detail serves as a roadmap for monitoring and establishing clear benchmarks against which progress can be measured.

A structured approach to monitoring involves regular check-ins or follow-up meetings. These sessions allow participants to report on their progress, discuss obstacles, and receive feedback. For students, these check-ins might be facilitated by counselors or peer mediators who can offer guidance and support. A designated administrator or human resources personnel might oversee the process for staff conflicts. Consistent and open communication ensures all parties remain engaged and committed to the agreement's success.

Documentation plays a pivotal role in monitoring the implementation of agreements. Keeping detailed records of progress, challenges, and any modifications to the deal ensures transparency and accountability. This record can be examined in follow-up meetings, giving debates a factual foundation and assisting in monitoring the resolution's long-term effects.

Involving all parties in monitoring is essential for maintaining trust and cooperation. Participants should be able to voice their opinions about the implementation's progress and weigh in on any choices regarding agreement modifications. This inclusive approach ensures that the monitoring process is fair and equitable and reinforces the participants' ownership of the resolution.

Adaptability is a critical aspect of effective monitoring. Conflicts and the needs of those involved can evolve, and the agreement may need to be adjusted to remain effective. Being open to modifying in response to feedback or changing circumstances demonstrates a commitment to the resolution's success and the parties' well-being.

Celebrating milestones and successes as part of the monitoring process can provide positive reinforcement and encourage continued adherence to the agreement. Recognizing participants' efforts and the progress made toward resolving the conflict can bolster morale and foster a sense of achievement. These celebrations can be simple acknowledgments in follow-up meetings or more formal recognitions, depending on the context.

The insights gained from monitoring the implementation of agreements can inform future conflict resolution efforts. Educational institutions can refine their conflict resolution policies and practices by analyzing what worked well, what challenges arose, and how they were addressed. This continuous learning and improvement cycle enhances the overall effectiveness of conflict resolution in the school, contributing to a more harmonious and supportive educational environment.

Monitoring the implementation of agreements is a vital component of the conflict resolution process in educational settings. Through structured follow-ups, clear documentation, inclusive participation, adaptability, and the celebration of progress, schools can ensure that resolutions are implemented effectively and contribute to lasting positive change within the school community.

Providing Continuous Support and Resources to Prevent Future Conflicts

Providing continuous support and resources to prevent future conflicts is an essential strategy within educational settings, aiming to cultivate a proactive and preventative approach to conflict resolution. This ongoing support system encompasses various dimensions, including emotional and psychological support, educational initiatives, and structural changes, all designed to address the underlying causes of conflicts and to equip individuals with the skills necessary for constructive communication and problem-solving. By investing in such comprehensive support and resources, educational institutions can foster a positive and inclusive culture that mitigates conflicts and enhances the overall well-being and development of the school community.

Emotional and Psychological Support

Central to preventing future conflicts is addressing students' and staff's emotional and psychological well-being. Schools can provide this support by offering access to counseling services, peer support programs, and mental health resources. These services help individuals navigate personal challenges, manage stress, and process emotions healthily, reducing the likelihood of these issues manifesting as conflicts within the school environment. Moreover, fostering an atmosphere where seeking help is encouraged and stigma-free promotes a culture of care and understanding.

Conflict Resolution Education

Educational initiatives focused on teaching conflict resolution skills are crucial in equipping students and staff with the tools to navigate disagreements constructively. This can include curriculum integration, workshops, and training sessions covering active listening, empathy, negotiation, and mediation. By embedding these skills into the educational experience, schools prepare individuals to approach conflicts with a mindset of resolution and collaboration rather than confrontation.

Social and Emotional Learning (SEL)

Social and emotional learning programs are pivotal in developing effective interpersonal interactions and emotional regulation competencies. SEL curricula that emphasize self-awareness, self-management, social awareness, relationship skills, and responsible decision-making can significantly reduce conflict occurrence. These programs teach individuals not only how to understand and manage their emotions but also how to empathize with others, appreciate diverse perspectives, and engage in positive social interactions.

Inclusive and Equitable Practices

Preventing conflicts in schools requires establishing an inclusive and equal atmosphere. This involves actively eliminating discrimination, bias, and inequality within the school system, ensuring all students and staff feel valued and respected. Schools can implement diversity and inclusion training, review policies through an equity lens, and create forums for open dialogue on these issues. By addressing systemic inequalities and fostering a culture of respect and inclusion, schools can minimize the tensions that often lead to conflicts.

Strengthening Community Connections

Strengthening the connections between the school and the wider community can provide additional support and resources for preventing conflicts. Partnerships with local organizations, families, and community groups can bring in external perspectives, resources, and support systems that enhance the school's conflict prevention efforts. These partnerships can also facilitate community-based learning experiences that broaden students' understanding of cooperation, civic engagement, and social responsibility, reducing the propensity for conflicts.

Peer Mediation and Support Programs

Peer mediation and support programs leverage the influence and relatability of peers to address and prevent conflicts. Training students as peer mediators equips them with the skills to facilitate resolution processes among their classmates, often in ways that are more accessible and effective than interventions by adults. Peer support programs, where students provide emotional and social support to one another, can also play a significant role in creating a supportive school climate that preempts conflicts.

Regular Review and Adaptation of Policies and Practices

To ensure the effectiveness of support and resources for conflict prevention, schools must regularly review and adapt their policies and practices. This entails evaluating the results of current initiatives, getting input from the school community, and keeping up with the most recent findings and recommended procedures in conflict resolution and prevention. An ongoing commitment to improvement ensures that the school's efforts remain responsive to the community's evolving needs and are effective in preventing future conflicts.

Providing continuous support and resources to prevent future conflicts is a multifaceted approach that addresses the root causes of disputes and equips individuals with the skills necessary for constructive engagement. Educational institutions can foster a caring and welcoming environment through peer programs, community participation, emotional and psychological support, social and emotional learning, conflict resolution courses, inclusive practices, and regular policy reviews. This proactive and comprehensive strategy minimizes conflicts and contributes to the overall well-being, development, and cohesion of the school community, laying the foundation for a positive and productive educational experience.

Cultivating a Culture of Conflict Prevention and Transformation

Cultivating a culture of conflict prevention and transformation within educational settings requires a multifaceted approach beyond merely reacting to conflicts as they arise. Instead, it involves creating an environment that proactively addresses the underlying causes of disputes and fosters a community-wide commitment to constructive communication, empathy, and mutual respect. This culture not only minimizes the occurrence of conflicts but also transforms potential disputes into opportunities for learning, growth, and strengthening relationships. Achieving this cultural shift demands the involvement of all school community members, including students, educators, administrators, and parents, each playing a vital role in promoting a more peaceful, inclusive, and supportive educational environment.

Embedding Conflict Resolution in the Curriculum

Integrating conflict resolution practices and ideas into the curriculum helps foster a culture of conflict prevention and transformation. This can be achieved through dedicated courses, workshops, and activities that teach students the skills necessary for effective communication, active listening, empathy, negotiation, and mediation. By integrating these lessons into the regular curriculum, schools can ensure that students develop these critical life skills early, preparing them to handle disagreements constructively and contribute positively to their communities.

Promoting Social and Emotional Learning (SEL)

Social and Emotional Learning (SEL) programs are crucial for fostering the emotional intelligence and interpersonal skills underpinning a conflict prevention culture. Students who participate in SEL programs emphasizing social awareness, self-awareness, connection-building, and responsible decision-making will be equipped to comprehend and control their emotions, empathize with others, and have constructive social interactions. These skills reduce the likelihood of conflicts arising and enhance students' overall well-being and academic success.

Creating Inclusive and Equitable Environments

A culture of conflict prevention is inherently linked to creating inclusive and equitable school environments. Minimizing the tensions that can result in disputes requires addressing bias, discrimination, and inequality, regardless of the basis for the discrimination—race, ethnicity, gender, sexual orientation, or any other feature. Schools can take proactive steps by implementing diversity and inclusion training, reviewing policies through an equity lens, and creating spaces for open dialogue about these issues. By valuing and respecting diversity within the school community, schools can foster a sense of belonging and mutual respect that significantly reduces the incidence of conflicts.

Encouraging Student Leadership and Participation

Empowering students to take on leadership roles in conflict prevention and transformation initiatives can profoundly impact the school culture. Student-led programs, such as peer mediation, anti-bullying campaigns, and restorative justice circles, allow students to apply conflict resolution skills in real-world contexts and to model positive behaviors for their peers. These programs provide practical experience in handling disputes and promote a sense of ownership and responsibility among students for maintaining a peaceful school environment.

Engaging Families and the Wider Community

The engagement of families and the wider community is critical for reinforcing the culture of conflict prevention beyond the school gates. Schools can collaborate with parents, local organizations, and community leaders to extend conflict resolution education and initiatives into the home and community. Workshops for parents, community service projects, and partnerships with local organizations can all contribute to a broader culture of peace and constructive communication.

Fostering Continuous Learning and Improvement

Finally, cultivating a culture of conflict prevention and transformation requires an ongoing commitment to learning and improvement. Regular training for educators, administrators, and staff in the latest conflict resolution and SEL practices ensures that the adults in the school community are equipped to effectively model and teach these principles. Additionally, schools can modify and improve their conflict prevention strategies to better serve their communities' changing requirements because of the ongoing assessment of their programs and policies, guided by input from families, staff, and students.

Cultivating a culture of conflict prevention and transformation in educational settings involves a comprehensive and proactive approach that addresses conflict's emotional, social, and ethical dimensions. Through education, inclusion, empowerment, community engagement, and continuous improvement, schools can create environments where conflicts are minimized and transformed into opportunities for positive change. This culture contributes to a more peaceful and supportive educational experience and equips students with the skills and values they need to thrive in an increasingly complex and diverse world.

Lessons Learned: Reflecting on the Resolution Process for Improvement

Reflecting on the resolution process for improvement is vital to any conflict resolution strategy within educational settings. This reflective practice involves thoroughly examining the entire conflict resolution journey—from the initial identification of the conflict to the implementation of the resolution and beyond. Schools can glean valuable lessons that inform future practices by analyzing what worked, what didn't, and why. This ensures that each conflict resolution experience contributes to developing more effective strategies and a stronger, more cohesive school community.

The Importance of Reflection

Reflection allows educators, mediators, and all parties involved in the conflict resolution process to step back and evaluate the effectiveness of their approaches. This assessment is essential for determining the short- and long-term effects of conflict resolution on the parties involved as well as the overall culture of the institution. Reflection fosters a culture of continuous learning, encouraging educators and students alike to grow from their experiences and to apply these lessons in future interactions.

Gathering Comprehensive Feedback

A thorough reflection on the resolution process begins with gathering feedback from all participants involved in the conflict. This information, which can be gathered through focus groups, interviews, or surveys, provides a range of perspectives on the procedure's benefits and drawbacks. Involving all parties in this feedback process enriches the reflection with multiple viewpoints and reinforces the value of each person's experience and opinion, fostering a sense of inclusion and respect.

Analyzing the Conflict Resolution Journey

Analyzing the conflict resolution journey involves examining each phase of the process, from the initial recognition of the conflict to the post-resolution follow-up. Key questions to consider include: How effectively were the root causes of the conflict identified? Were all parties given an equal opportunity to voice their concerns? How well did the chosen resolution strategies address the needs and interests of those involved? Were there any unintended consequences of the resolution? How effective was the follow-up and support provided to the parties post-resolution? This comprehensive analysis helps identify specific areas for improvement and highlights practices that should be continued or adapted.

Identifying Patterns and Trends

Beyond analyzing individual conflicts, reflecting on the resolution process can reveal patterns and trends within the school's approach to conflict resolution. Are certain types of disputes occurring more frequently? Are there recurring challenges in the resolution process? Identifying these patterns can help schools proactively address systemic issues, whether through policy changes, support system enhancements, or educational environment modifications.

Learning from Successes and Challenges

Every conflict resolution process, regardless of its outcome, offers valuable lessons. Successes highlight effective strategies and practices that can be replicated in future conflicts, serving as models for best practices within the school. Conversely, challenges provide opportunities for growth and innovation, prompting schools to explore new approaches and strengthen existing practices. Schools can openly discuss successes and challenges and create a learning environment that values improvement and resilience.

Implementing Changes Based on Reflection

The ultimate goal of reflecting on the resolution process is implementing changes that enhance the school's conflict resolution capabilities. This might involve revising conflict resolution policies, introducing new training programs for students and staff, or adopting new approaches to foster a more positive school climate. Implementing these changes requires commitment from all levels of the school community, from administrators to students, and should be guided by inclusivity, equity, and continuous improvement.

Fostering a Culture of Reflection

To maximize the benefits of reflection, schools should foster a culture that values and encourages ongoing evaluation and learning. This can be achieved by integrating reflective practices into regular school activities, providing training on reflective techniques, and creating spaces where students and staff feel safe to share their experiences and insights. A culture of reflection enhances the effectiveness of conflict resolution efforts and contributes to the overall growth and development of the school community.

Reflecting on the resolution process for improvement is a crucial strategy for enhancing conflict resolution practices within educational settings. By systematically evaluating the resolution journey, gathering comprehensive feedback, analyzing successes and challenges, and implementing informed changes, schools can continuously refine their approaches to conflict resolution. This reflective practice leads to more effective and sustainable resolutions. It fosters a culture of continuous learning, improvement, and resilience, laying the foundation for a more harmonious and supportive educational environment.

Reintegration Strategies for Conflict Parties within the Educational Environment

Reintegration strategies for conflict parties within the educational environment are crucial for restoring harmony and ensuring that all individuals involved can participate fully and positively in the school community. Regardless of their nature, conflicts can lead to divisions, hurt feelings, and alienation. Effective reintegration strategies address these issues head-on, focusing on healing, rebuilding trust, and fostering a sense of belonging. These strategies are about resolving the immediate conflict and transforming the post-conflict environment into one that supports the growth, learning, and well-being of every student and staff member.

Creating a Supportive Reintegration Plan

The foundation of successful reintegration is a well-crafted plan tailored to the specific needs of the parties involved and the broader school community. This plan should outline the steps for reintegration, including any necessary support services, activities designed to rebuild relationships, and mechanisms for ongoing monitoring and support. The development of this plan should involve input from the conflict parties, educators, counselors, and, if appropriate, family members, ensuring that it addresses the concerns and needs of all stakeholders.

Facilitating Healing and Forgiveness

Central to the reintegration process is facilitating healing and forgiveness among the conflict parties. This may involve structured dialogue sessions where individuals can express their feelings, share their experiences, and offer apologies. Training facilitators should guide such sessions, ensuring the dialogue remains constructive and respectful. Additionally, activities that promote empathy and understanding, such as restorative circles or shared projects, can help mend relationships and foster a sense of mutual forgiveness.

Providing Emotional and Psychological Support

Conflicts can have a significant emotional and psychological impact, necessitating ongoing support for those involved. Peer support groups, counseling programs, and other mental health resources should be accessible in schools to assist students in processing their experiences and creating suitable coping mechanisms. This support should be readily accessible and confidential, encouraging students and staff to seek help without fear of stigma or judgment.

Ensuring Academic and Social Support

Reintegration after a conflict may also require academic and social support, particularly if the conflict leads to disruptions in learning or changes in social dynamics. Academic support might include tutoring, adjustments to workload, or alternative learning arrangements to help students catch up and succeed. Social support could involve:

- Facilitating re-entry into peer groups.
- Creating inclusive activities that encourage positive social interactions.
- Providing mentorship programs to guide students in navigating the social aspects of school life.

Promoting Positive School Climate

For successful reintegration, schools must have a welcoming and supportive atmosphere. Schools should actively promote values such as respect, empathy, and kindness, creating an environment where all members feel valued and supported. This can be achieved through school-wide initiatives, such as anti-bullying campaigns, diversity and inclusion programs, and community service projects that encourage students and staff to work together towards common goals and appreciate the strength of their diversity.

Monitoring Progress and Adjusting Support as Needed

Effective reintegration requires ongoing monitoring to assess the conflict parties' progress and the school community's overall health. Regular check-ins with the individuals involved and with educators and counselors can provide valuable insights into how the reintegration is progressing and whether additional support or adjustments are needed. This monitoring should be conducted with sensitivity and confidentiality, ensuring the parties feel supported rather than scrutinized.

Fostering Leadership and Peer Support

Encouraging leadership and peer support among students can significantly enhance successful reintegration. By providing direction and encouragement to their fellow students, peer leaders and mediators can act as positive role models for their peers. By empowering students to promote a positive school culture and actively support their peers, schools can cultivate an environment of mutual care and respect that significantly enhances reintegration.

Reintegration strategies for conflict parties within the educational environment are essential for healing divisions, rebuilding trust, and ensuring all individuals can thrive post-conflict. Educational institutions can effectively navigate reintegration challenges by implementing a comprehensive approach that includes emotional and psychological support, academic and social assistance, and initiatives to promote a positive school climate. Such strategies benefit those directly involved in the conflict and enhance the overall well-being and cohesion of the school community, creating an environment where learning, growth, and positive relationships can flourish.

Developing Policies and Procedures Based on Post-Conflict Insights

Developing policies and procedures based on post-conflict insights is a forward-thinking approach that schools can adopt to enhance their conflict resolution framework. This strategy involves reflecting on the lessons learned from past conflicts, analyzing their root causes, the effectiveness of the resolution strategies employed, and the overall impact on the school community. By doing so, educational institutions can establish a robust set of policies and procedures that not only prevent future conflicts but also ensure that when disputes arise, they are managed in a constructive, equitable, and conducive to the long-term well-being of all involved.

Gathering Comprehensive Insights

The first step in developing these policies and procedures is gathering insights from past conflicts. This involves collecting feedback from students, teachers, administrators, and parents involved in or affected by conflicts. Surveys, interviews, and focus groups can be practical tools for understanding the diverse perspectives and experiences within the school community. Furthermore, reviewing the disputes' records and how they were resolved might yield important information about patterns and trends that might not be immediately clear from individual stories.

Analyzing Conflict Dynamics

With a comprehensive dataset, the next step is to analyze the dynamics of past conflicts. The common causes of disagreements, workable solutions, and the effects of the resolutions on the relationships between the parties and the larger school community should be the main topics of this investigation. Particular attention should be paid to any systemic issues that may have contributed to conflicts, such as policies that inadvertently create inequities or communication breakdowns that exacerbate misunderstandings.

Incorporating Restorative Practices

One critical insight that may emerge from the analysis is the effectiveness of restorative practices in conflict resolution. Schools that successfully employ therapeutic approaches, such as mediation, peace circles, or reconciliation programs, can codify these practices into their policies and procedures. This codification formalizes the commitment to restorative justice and provides a clear framework for its implementation, ensuring consistency and accessibility across the school.

Enhancing Communication Channels

Effective communication is often at the heart of both the cause and resolution of conflicts. Insights from past conflicts can highlight the need for improved communication channels within the school. Policies and procedures developed in response may include regular open forums for students and staff to voice concerns, enhanced protocols for parent-teacher communication, and clear guidelines for how and when to escalate issues to administrators. Schools can prevent misunderstandings and grievances from escalating into more significant conflicts by prioritizing open and transparent communication.

Fostering a Positive School Culture

The insights gained from analyzing past conflicts can also inform policies fostering a positive school culture. These policies might focus on promoting inclusivity, respect, and empathy as core values of the school community. Initiatives could include:

- Diversity and inclusion training.
- Social and emotional learning programs.
- Community-building activities that encourage collaboration and mutual understanding among students and staff.

Educational institutions can establish a climate in which conflicts are less likely to occur and more likely to be resolved amicably when they do by integrating these ideals into the very fabric of the school.

Implementing Preventative Measures

Preventing conflicts before they occur is an ideal outcome for any educational institution. Based on the insights gathered, schools can develop policies and procedures that proactively address the conditions that lead to disputes. This might involve revising disciplinary policies to be more equitable, implementing bullying prevention programs, or adjusting academic policies to reduce student stress and competition. These preventative efforts improve the school community's general health and happiness, which also lessen the likelihood of confrontations.

Establishing Continuous Learning and Improvement Processes

Finally, recognizing that conflict resolution is an evolving field, policies, and procedures should include ongoing learning and improvement mechanisms. This can be accomplished by providing staff members with professional development opportunities to improve their conflict resolution abilities, reviewing conflict resolution results regularly, and updating policies in light of new research and best practices. By committing to continuous learning and adaptation, schools can ensure that their conflict resolution framework remains effective, responsive, and aligned with the needs of their community.

Developing policies and procedures based on post-conflict insights is a strategic approach that enables educational institutions to enhance their conflict resolution capabilities. By reflecting on past conflicts, analyzing their dynamics, and implementing targeted improvements, schools can not only better manage disputes but also foster a school culture that is more inclusive, communicative, and supportive. This proactive and reflective strategy not only addresses the immediate challenges of conflict resolution but also contributes to the long-term well-being and development of the school community, laying the groundwork for a more harmonious educational environment.

Community Engagement and Support in Post-Conflict Recovery

Community engagement and support play pivotal roles in the post-conflict recovery process within educational settings, emphasizing the collective responsibility and contribution towards healing and rebuilding after disputes. In the aftermath of conflicts, the school community—encompassing students, educators, administrators, parents, and local organizations—faces the task of addressing the immediate outcomes of disputes and fostering an environment that prevents recurrence and promotes lasting peace. Engaging the broader community in the recovery process leverages diverse resources and perspectives and strengthens the social fabric, ensuring a more resilient and supportive educational environment for all.

Harnessing Local Expertise and Resources

Community engagement in post-conflict recovery involves harnessing local expertise and resources for mutual benefit. This could mean collaborating with mental health professionals to provide counseling services, partnering with local peace-building organizations for workshops, or engaging community leaders in dialogue initiatives. These partnerships enrich the support network available to the school, offering specialized services and interventions that might be beyond the school's capabilities and embedding the educational institution more firmly within the community ecosystem.

Facilitating Parent and Guardian Involvement

Parents and guardians are crucial allies in the post-conflict recovery process. Their involvement ensures that the efforts initiated within the school extend into the home, providing a consistent and supportive environment for affected individuals. Schools can facilitate this involvement by organizing informational sessions that equip parents with conflict resolution and communication skills, creating forums for parents to share experiences and strategies, and establishing clear channels for ongoing communication between the school and families. This collaborative approach not only aids in the recovery process but also fosters a sense of shared responsibility and partnership.

Student-Led Initiatives

Empowering students to lead and participate in post-conflict recovery efforts is a powerful method of community engagement. Student-led initiatives, such as peer mediation programs, anti-bullying campaigns, and diversity clubs, provide valuable support services and cultivate leadership skills and a sense of agency among students. These initiatives encourage a proactive stance towards conflict prevention and resolution, demonstrating to students that they play a critical role in shaping their school's culture.

Promoting Community Cohesion through Shared Activities

Shared community activities that transcend the school boundaries can significantly contribute to post-conflict recovery by promoting cohesion and mutual understanding. These activities include community service projects, inter-school competitions, cultural events, or joint workshops on topics of mutual interest. Such initiatives provide opportunities for positive interactions and collaboration, breaking down barriers and fostering a sense of unity and shared purpose.

Utilizing Restorative Justice Approaches

Incorporating restorative justice approaches into community engagement can facilitate more profound healing and reconciliation. By involving the immediate parties to the conflict and the wider community in restorative practices, schools can address the broader impact of conflicts and work towards collective solutions. Community circles, restorative dialogues, and community service projects can all serve as platforms for restorative justice, emphasizing healing, accountability, and the restoration of relationships.

Continuous Feedback and Involvement in Policy Development

Engaging the community in continuous feedback and involvement in policy development ensures that the strategies adopted for post-conflict recovery and prevention are responsive to the community's needs. This can be achieved through regular surveys, community forums, and participation in school governance. Such inclusive practices ensure that the voices of all stakeholders are heard and considered in developing policies and programs, building a more vital, cohesive community ethos.

Celebrating Progress and Successes Together

Finally, celebrating progress and successes as a community can reinforce the positive outcomes of post-conflict recovery efforts and motivate continued collaboration and support. Acknowledging the contributions of students, staff, parents, and community partners in healing and rebuilding after conflicts provides recognition and appreciation and highlight collective achievements in creating a peaceful and supportive educational environment.

Community engagement and support are indispensable in the post-conflict recovery process within educational settings. By leveraging local expertise, facilitating parental involvement, empowering student-led initiatives, promoting community cohesion, utilizing restorative practices, involving the community in policy development, and celebrating successes, schools can recover from conflicts and build a foundation for lasting peace and resilience. This cooperative strategy emphasizes the value of working together to overcome obstacles and create a climate in which all school community members can flourish.

CHAPTER 7

DIGITAL AGE CONFLICTS

Cyberbullying is when someone uses the internet, a cellphone, or other technology to hurt, embarrass, or intimidate someone else. It's a big problem in schools today because almost every student uses technology for learning and socializing. Understanding cyberbullying's causes and effects and how to resolve it is crucial for creating safer online environments for everyone.

Causes of Cyberbullying

1. Anonymity: Many cyberbullies hide behind anonymous profiles, thinking they won't get caught.
2. Power: Some people bully others online to feel powerful or in control.
3. Lack of Awareness: Sometimes, individuals don't realize the impact of their words or actions online.
4. Following Others: Some might start cyberbullying because they see their friends doing it or to fit in with a particular group.

Effects of Cyberbullying

1. Emotional Distress: Victims often feel sad, scared, or embarrassed. This can lead to them avoiding school or social activities.
2. Lower Self-esteem: Being bullied online can make someone feel bad about themselves and doubt their worth.

3. Problems at School: Victims might struggle with schoolwork, have trouble focusing, or even skip school because they feel unsafe.
4. Health Issues: The stress from cyberbullying can lead to headaches, stomachaches, and mental health problems like anxiety or depression.

Resolution Strategies

1. Education: Teaching students, parents, and teachers about cyberbullying and its effects is the first step in prevention. Awareness campaigns can help everyone recognize and stand up against cyberbullying.
2. Open Communication: Encourage students to talk about their online experiences and tell an adult if they or someone they know is cyberbullied.
3. Promote empathy: Help students understand how their actions affect others. Encouraging empathy can make them think twice before posting harmful messages.
4. Set Rules and Consequences: Schools should have clear rules about cyberbullying and what will happen if someone breaks these rules. This shows that cyberbullying is taken seriously.
5. Use Technology Solutions: Most social media platforms have tools and settings that can help block or report cyberbullying. Teaching students and parents these tools can empower them to protect themselves online.
6. Support Systems: Support victims and bullies. Counseling can help victims cope with the effects of cyberbullying. Bullies often need help dealing with the problems that lead them to hurt others.
7. Community Efforts: Work with parents, local organizations, and law enforcement to create a community-wide approach to combat cyberbullying. This

can include workshops, parent meetings, and community service projects.

Creating a culture of respect and kindness online is essential. By understanding cyberbullying's causes and effects and implementing effective resolution strategies, schools can help ensure that the internet is safe for all students to learn, share, and connect.

Managing Social Media Disputes: Guidelines for Educators and Students

Managing social media disputes requires careful consideration, especially in educational settings where the line between personal and public can often blur. Social media platforms, while offering vast opportunities for learning and connection, can also become arenas for conflicts among students and sometimes between students and educators. To navigate these waters smoothly, educators and students must adopt guidelines that promote respectful interaction, protect privacy, and ensure a positive online environment.

Teachers are essential in setting an example of proper online conduct. They should demonstrate professionalism and courtesy in their social media interactions as they would in the classroom. This includes respecting the privacy of students and colleagues, avoiding the public discussion of sensitive issues, and being mindful of the content they share or endorse. Teachers can also assist children in comprehending the significance of keeping a positive digital footprint and the consequences of their activities online.

Teaching students to behave politely and respectfully online and in person is essential. This includes thinking carefully before posting or sharing content that could be hurtful or harmful to others, respecting others' privacy by not sharing personal information without consent, and being open to different perspectives without resorting to aggression or bullying.

When disputes arise on social media, educators and students need to approach resolution with a focus on understanding and empathy. Engaging in a private online discussion yields less fruitful results than taking the discussion outside and addressing the problem more intimately. This offers a chance to resolve any underlying issues that have fueled the argument and to move toward understanding between the parties.

Preventive education about social media's potential pitfalls is also crucial. Frequent dialogues, seminars, and even curricular integration can help students think critically about the material they access and share online. To establish a shared set of social media standards and norms for their school community, educators can work with students to emphasize the virtues of accountability, respect, and honesty.

Both educators and students should be familiar with the tools and options available on social media platforms for managing privacy settings, reporting harassment, and blocking users who engage in inappropriate behavior. Understanding these tools empowers individuals to protect themselves and others from online harm.

Establishing a safe space where students feel at ease talking about their online experiences and any problems they encounter is essential. Schools should have clear policies in place for addressing social media disputes that involve bullying or harassment, including procedures for reporting, investigation, and resolution. These rules must undergo periodic reviews and updates to align with the dynamic digital environment.

Managing social media disputes effectively requires a collaborative effort between educators and students, grounded in mutual respect, open communication, and a commitment to creating a positive online community. By setting clear expectations, modeling appropriate behavior, and providing education and support, schools can help ensure that social media remains a space for safe, respectful, and enriching interaction.

Digital Literacy and Conflict Resolution

Digital literacy and conflict resolution are critical skills for students in today's technology-driven world. Digital literacy requires knowing how to utilize technology responsibly and safely. Conflict resolution involves finding peaceful solutions to disagreements. Together, these skills help students navigate online spaces more effectively, reducing the risk of conflicts and knowing how to handle them when they arise.

Why Digital Literacy Matters

Digital literacy means being aware of the consequences of our online behavior in addition to being able to operate devices and apps. It teaches students to think before they click, share, or post. This is important because what we do online can affect us and others. For example, sharing someone else's personal information without their permission can hurt that person. Digital literacy helps students understand these consequences, making them more careful and respectful online.

Conflict Resolution Online

Conflicts can quickly happen online because it's harder to understand each other without seeing faces or hearing voices. Sometimes, a message meant as a joke might upset someone. Learning conflict resolution helps students deal with these situations calmly and constructively. They learn to listen to each other's viewpoints, explain their feelings without accusing, and find solutions that work for everyone. This way, minor misunderstandings don't turn into big arguments.

Critical Skills for Digital Literacy and Conflict Resolution

1. Empathy: Understanding how someone else feels is a big part of using the internet wisely and resolving conflicts. Empathy helps students think about how their words and actions affect others, leading to kinder interactions.

2. Critical Thinking: Students must critically evaluate information and situations. This means not believing everything they see online and thinking about how to respond to disagreements.

3. Communication: Clear and respectful communication is critical. Students acquire clear communication of ideas and attentive listening skills, which are valuable in both online and offline contexts.

4. Privacy: Understanding privacy helps students protect their information and respect others' privacy. This reduces the chance of conflicts over shared information.

5. Problem-Solving: Being able to solve problems is crucial. Students can resolve conflicts without hurting relationships When they know how to negotiate and find solutions.

How to Teach These Skills

Educators can teach these skills through regular discussions, activities, and lessons that involve real-life scenarios students might face online. Role-playing exercises that simulate online interactions can be efficient. Schools can also use digital platforms designed for education to provide students with hands-on experience in a controlled environment.

Incorporating parents and guardians in the learning process can extend these lessons beyond the classroom. Workshops or information sessions can equip parents with the knowledge to support their children's digital literacy and conflict-resolution skills at home.

Finally, creating a school culture that values kindness, respect, and open communication reinforces these skills daily. Celebrating examples of positive online behavior and successful conflict resolution can motivate students to apply what they've learned.

Equipping students with digital literacy and conflict resolution skills is essential for navigating the online world safely and respectfully. By focusing on empathy, critical thinking, clear communication, privacy, and problem-solving, educators can confidently prepare students to face the challenges of the digital age. This enhances their online experiences and teaches valuable life skills that will serve them well into the future.

Safeguarding Privacy and Data in Schools: Conflict Prevention Measures

Safeguarding privacy and data in schools is essential for preventing conflicts. With so much school work happening online, keeping personal information and data safe helps everyone feel more secure and avoids problems. Let's discuss how schools can protect privacy and data and why it's an excellent way to stop conflicts before they start.

Understanding Privacy and Data

First, knowing what we mean by privacy and data is essential. Privacy means keeping personal information safe, like your name, where you live, and your phone number. Data can be anything from your grades to what you search for on the internet to the emails you send. In schools, protecting this information helps students and teachers feel safe and respected.

Why It's Important

When privacy and data are not protected, it can lead to trouble. For example, if someone's personal information is shared without permission, they might feel embarrassed or upset. It can also lead to more significant problems, like bullying or identity theft. That's why schools need good rules and systems to keep everyone's information safe.

Conflict Prevention Measures

Here are some ways schools can help protect privacy and data, which also helps stop conflicts:

1. Education: Teaching students and staff about why privacy matters and how to stay safe online is a significant first step. This can include learning about solid passwords, thinking carefully before sharing personal information, and knowing what to do if your privacy has been violated.

2. Clear Rules: Schools should have clear rules about using and sharing personal information and data. Everyone should know these rules and understand why they're essential.

3. Safe Technology: Schools can use technology with reasonable security measures to protect data. This includes secure internet connections, protected databases for storing information, and tools that help keep harmful people or software away.

4. Regular Checks: Schools should regularly check their systems to ensure they're still safe and fix any problems immediately. This is like locking the doors and windows to keep everyone safe inside.

5. A Plan for Problems: Even with the best plans, problems can still happen. Schools should have a plan for what to do if privacy or data is compromised. This can help solve the problem quickly and prevent it from getting more significant.

6. Listening and Support: Schools should listen and provide support if someone feels their privacy violated. This shows that the school takes their concerns seriously and is there to help.

Benefits of Protecting Privacy and Data

When schools do an excellent job of protecting privacy and data, it creates a safer and more respectful environment for everyone. Teachers and students can concentrate on teaching and learning without worrying about personal information. It also builds trust within the school community, as everyone knows their information is handled carefully.

Protecting privacy and data in schools is not just about using the right technology or having rules. It's about creating a culture of respect and safety that values everyone's right to privacy. By safeguarding this information, schools can prevent conflicts and ensure everyone feels safe and respected. This is important for building a positive and productive learning environment where everyone can succeed.

Cultivating Digital Empathy

Cultivating digital empathy is all about teaching and encouraging kindness in the online world. Like in real life, being kind and understanding how others feel can make a big difference in how we get along online. Digital empathy means recognizing that there's a natural person with feelings behind every screen. This understanding can lead to more thoughtful interactions, less bullying, and a friendlier online community. Let's explore why digital empathy is essential and how we can all help to foster it.

In the digital age, we spend much time online, whether for school, work, or fun. Sometimes, it's easy to forget that our words and actions on the internet can affect people just as much as if we were face-to-face. Have you ever read a mean comment and felt hurt? Or maybe you've seen someone else picked on online and felt terrible for them. That's where digital empathy comes in. It's about stopping to think about how your words can make someone else feel before you hit send.

One way to encourage digital empathy is through education. Children can hear from parents and teachers about being responsible digital citizens. This includes being respectful, thinking before posting, and understanding that our online actions have real-world consequences. It's also about teaching kids to stand up for others. Suppose you see someone being bullied online or something doesn't feel right. In that case, it's essential to speak up, whether telling an adult, using online tools to report bullying, or simply offering kind words to the targeted person.

Another crucial part of cultivating digital empathy is setting a good example. Adults can set an example by being aware of their digital footprint and acting kindly in online interactions. Remember, young eyes are watching and learning from everything we do online.

Encouraging kindness online also means creating spaces where everyone feels welcome and safe. Schools and communities can set up online forums or social media groups that promote positive interactions and support those struggling. These spaces can be places where students share their experiences, offer advice, and celebrate each other's successes—all done with kindness and empathy.

Sometimes, we all need reminders that there's a person on the other side of the screen. Activities that help build empathy, like reading stories or watching videos about people from different backgrounds and experiences, can open our eyes to other perspectives. Understanding that everyone has their own story can make us think twice before we post something hurtful.

Finally, fostering digital empathy is about building a culture of support and understanding. It's about making the online world a kinder place where everyone feels like they belong and where differences are celebrated, not attacked. This doesn't happen overnight, but we can make a big difference with everyone playing their part—students, teachers, parents, and online communities.

Cultivating digital empathy is crucial in today's digital world. We can foster a more understanding, polite, and sympathetic online community by modeling and promoting kindness online. This starts with education, setting a good example, creating supportive spaces, seeking to understand different perspectives, and building a culture of kindness. Together, we can make the online world a better place for everyone.

Conflict Resolution Tools for the Digital World

In today's digital world, technology plays a significant role in communicating and resolving conflicts. With the rise of social media and online interactions, new challenges in conflict resolution have emerged. However, technology also offers innovative solutions. Now, apps and platforms are designed specifically to help manage and resolve conflicts in digital spaces. These tools can be handy for students, educators, and anyone navigating the complexities of online communication.

Mediation Apps

Mediation apps are designed to facilitate the resolution process by providing a structured environment for discussion. These apps often include features like guided communication prompts, which help keep conversations constructive and focused on resolution.

Some apps also offer the option of involving a neutral third party to mediate the discussion, ensuring that all sides are heard fairly. This can be particularly useful when emotions run high and a calm, neutral perspective is needed.

Emotional Intelligence (EQ) Tools

Understanding and managing emotions is critical to effective conflict resolution. Platforms and apps now offer training in emotional intelligence (EQ), providing users with strategies for recognizing their feelings and responding to the emotions of others constructively. These tools often include interactive exercises, videos, and quizzes that help build empathy, self-regulation, and practical communication skills. By enhancing emotional intelligence, individuals can better navigate conflicts when they arise.

Online Forums and Support Groups

Sometimes, talking about a conflict with others who understand can be incredibly helpful. Online forums and support groups provide places for people to talk about their experiences, ask for guidance, and lend a hand to those going through a similar situation. These platforms help people feel like they belong to a community. This is particularly beneficial when resolving conflicts because it lets people know they're not alone in their experiences.

Collaborative Problem-Solving Platforms

Collaborative problem-solving platforms are designed to help groups work together to find solutions to conflicts or challenges. These tools often feature shared digital workspaces where users can post ideas, vote on solutions, and track progress toward resolution. By encouraging collaborative rather than confrontational approaches to conflict, these platforms can foster a more cooperative and positive online environment.

Feedback and Survey Tools

Gathering feedback is an essential part of resolving conflicts and improving relationships. Feedback and survey tools allow individuals or organizations to collect anonymous feedback about a conflict or issue, providing insights into the perspectives and feelings of all parties involved. This information can be invaluable for understanding a conflict's root causes and developing strategies to address it effectively.

Peer Mediation Networks

Peer mediation networks leverage the power of peer support to help resolve conflicts among students or young people. These networks train students to act as mediators, providing a relatable and accessible resource for their peers navigating conflicts. By promoting peer-led resolution, these networks empower young people to create a more peaceful and supportive community actively.

Restorative Justice Apps

Restorative justice focuses on healing and making amends rather than punishment. Now, apps are dedicated to facilitating restorative justice processes, guiding users through steps like acknowledging harm, communicating impact, and agreeing on restorative actions. These apps help ensure the process is consistent and meaningful for all parties involved.

Conflict resolution tools for the digital world offer innovative and accessible ways to manage disputes in online spaces. Technology provides new avenues for understanding, communication, and resolution, from mediation apps to emotional intelligence tools and peer mediation networks. By leveraging these tools, individuals and communities can work towards more constructive and empathetic approaches to resolving conflicts in the digital age.

Policy Development for Digital Conflict Management and Prevention

In today's educational environments, where digital contacts are essential to daily life, policy formulation for digital conflict prevention and management is critical. Creating clear, comprehensive policies helps schools navigate online conflicts effectively, ensuring a safe and respectful online environment for all school community members. These policies set the expectations for behavior, outline the steps for addressing digital conflicts, and provide a framework for preventive measures, all aimed at fostering a positive digital culture.

Establishing Clear Guidelines

The first step in policy development is establishing clear guidelines for acceptable online behavior. These guidelines should cover various aspects of digital interaction, including communication on social media platforms, email etiquette, and the appropriate use of school technology resources. By clearly defining what is considered respectful and responsible behavior online, schools can set the tone for digital interactions and provide a benchmark against which actions can be measured.

Incorporating Digital Citizenship Education

Digital citizenship education is vital for equipping students with the knowledge and skills to navigate the online world safely and respectfully. Effective policies should incorporate digital citizenship into the curriculum, covering topics such as online safety, privacy protection, the impact of digital footprints, and strategies for dealing with cyberbullying. This education empowers students to make informed decisions online and understand the consequences of their digital actions.

130

Outlining Procedures for Reporting and Addressing Digital Conflicts

Policies must clearly outline the procedures for reporting digital conflicts or concerns. This includes specifying who students and staff should contact if they experience online harassment, bullying, or other forms of digital conflict. Additionally, the policy should detail the steps the school will take to investigate and address reported issues, including timelines, confidentiality measures, and the criteria for involving external authorities if necessary.

Implementing Preventive Measures

Prevention is critical to managing digital conflicts effectively. Policies should outline preventive measures such as regular monitoring of school-owned digital platforms, filtering and blocking software to prevent access to harmful content, and establishing a digital monitoring team. Preventive measures include promoting a positive online culture through school-wide initiatives encouraging kindness, empathy, and respect in digital interactions.

Providing Support and Resources

Recognizing that digital conflicts can have significant emotional and psychological effects, policies should include provisions for support and resources for those affected. This can involve access to counseling services, peer support programs, and educational resources for rebuilding digital reputations. Providing support not only aids in the recovery process but also reinforces the school's commitment to the well-being of its community members.

Encouraging Community Involvement

Effective digital conflict management and prevention require the involvement of the entire school community, including students, staff, and parents. Policies should encourage community involvement through regular communication, workshops, and forums that educate all stakeholders about digital safety and the school's policies. Engaging the community fosters a collaborative approach to creating a safe and respectful digital environment.

Reviewing and Updating Policies Regularly

The digital landscape constantly evolves, with new platforms, trends, and challenges regularly emerging. Therefore, schools must periodically review and update their digital conflict management and prevention policies. This ensures policies remain relevant and effective in addressing digital challenges and incorporating the latest best practices in digital safety and citizenship.

Policy development for digital conflict management and prevention is essential to creating safe, respectful, and positive digital environments in educational settings. By establishing clear guidelines, incorporating digital citizenship education, outlining reporting and resolution procedures, implementing preventive measures, providing support, encouraging community involvement, and committing to regular policy reviews, schools can effectively manage digital conflicts and promote a culture of responsible and empathetic digital interaction.

CHAPTER 8

PSYCHOLOGICAL ASPECTS OF CONFLICT

Emotional intelligence (EQ) is crucial in understanding and navigating conflict dynamics, especially in environments where interactions can significantly impact relationships, such as schools. The term emotional intelligence (EQ) describes the capacity to identify, comprehend, regulate, and constructively utilize one's emotions to reduce stress, communicate clearly, sympathize with others, overcome obstacles, and diffuse conflict. This skill set is precious in conflict situations, influencing the outcome of disputes and how conflicts are perceived, approached, and resolved.

Understanding and Managing Emotions

One key component of emotional intelligence in conflict dynamics is the ability to understand and manage one's own emotions. Conflicts often evoke strong emotions, clouding judgment and leading to reactions that escalate the situation. Individuals with high EQ are better equipped to recognize their emotional responses, understand the triggers behind these emotions, and manage them effectively. This self-awareness and self-regulation allow for a more measured approach to conflict, where decisions are not driven by anger or frustration but by a conscious choice to seek resolution.

Empathy

Empathy, another critical aspect of emotional intelligence, involves understanding and sharing the feelings of others. In conflicts, empathy enables individuals to see the situation from the other person's perspective, fostering a deeper understanding of their motives, feelings, and reactions. This knowledge might change the emphasis from winning the debate to coming up with a solution that takes into account the wants and needs of each party. Empathy builds bridges, encouraging cooperation and collaboration rather than competition and antagonism.

Effective Communication

Emotional intelligence also enhances communication skills, which are essential for resolving conflicts. High-EQ individuals can articulate their thoughts and feelings clearly and listen actively to others, ensuring that communication is expressive and receptive. They are also adept at interpreting nonverbal clues, such as voice inflection and body language, which can reveal more about the emotions at work. Effective communication fosters a culture of free and honest discussion of problems without fear of reprisal or condemnation.

Problem-solving

Emotionally intelligent individuals approach conflict problem-solving with creativity and flexibility. They can think more clearly and evaluate many options because they can maintain composure under pressure, especially in emotionally intense situations. Moreover, their empathetic understanding of all parties' perspectives enables them to propose considerate and inclusive solutions, increasing the likelihood of a mutually satisfactory resolution.

Building and Maintaining Relationships

Ultimately, emotional intelligence's role in conflict dynamics extends beyond resolving specific disputes. High-EQ individuals are adept at using conflicts as opportunities for growth and learning, personally and within relationships. By addressing conflicts constructively, they can strengthen trust and respect between parties, laying the groundwork for more positive interactions in the future. Therefore, emotional intelligence not only facilitates the resolution of immediate conflicts but also contributes to the development of a more harmonious and supportive community.

Emotional intelligence significantly influences conflict dynamics. It offers tools for understanding and managing emotions, empathizing with others, communicating effectively, and solving problems creatively. These skills are invaluable in transforming conflicts from potential crises into opportunities for growth, understanding, and strengthening relationships. Cultivating emotional intelligence can lead to more constructive conflict resolution and a more supportive, engaged community in educational settings and beyond.

Stress and Anxiety as Drivers of Conflict

Stress and anxiety often lie at the heart of conflicts, acting as powerful drivers that can escalate disagreements into full-blown disputes. In educational settings, where pressures abound—from academic demands to social dynamics—recognizing and managing these emotional states can significantly reduce the incidence and intensity of conflicts. Teachers, staff, and students may all live in a more encouraging and peaceful atmosphere in schools if they recognize how stress and anxiety fuel conflict and take steps to resolve them.

Understanding the Link Between Stress, Anxiety, and Conflict

Stress and anxiety can distort perceptions, hinder communication, and provoke defensive or aggressive behavior, all of which can fuel conflicts. For instance, a stressed student may misinterpret a peer's

135

comment as hostile, leading to an unnecessary confrontation. Similarly, an anxious teacher might react disproportionately to minor disruptions. Recognizing these emotions as underlying conflict factors is the first step toward effective resolution.

Strategies for Identification

1. Observation and Awareness: Teachers and staff should receive training on how to spot stress and anxiety in both themselves and their students. These symptoms could be agitation, withdrawal, behavioral problems, or a drop in academic performance.

2. Open Communication Channels: Creating an environment where students and staff feel comfortable expressing their concerns and emotions can help identify stress and anxiety early on. Regular check-ins and supportive dialogues encourage individuals to speak up before tensions escalate.

3. Surveys and Feedback: Anonymous surveys can provide insights into the general well-being of the school community and help identify areas of concern that may contribute to stress and anxiety.

Management Strategies

1. Stress Reduction Programs: Schools can implement programs focused on stress reduction techniques, such as mindfulness, meditation, and time management skills. By giving participants the skills to control their tension and anxiety, these programs can lessen the chance of confrontation.

2. Support Services: Providing access to counseling and mental health services is crucial. By providing a secure environment for people to investigate and deal with the underlying reasons for their tension and anxiety, these services may be able to avoid confrontations.

3. Educational Workshops: Workshops that educate students and staff about the impact of stress and anxiety on behavior and relationships can foster a more understanding and empathetic school culture. This knowledge can prompt more compassionate responses in potentially tense situations.

4. Physical Activity and Recreation: Encouraging physical activity and providing recreation opportunities can help alleviate stress and anxiety. Sports, clubs, and creative arts programs can offer outlets for expression and relaxation.

5. Building a Supportive Community: Stress and anxiety can be lessened by fostering an atmosphere in schools that values acceptance, cooperation, and respect for one another. Peer support programs, mentorship, and team-building activities can strengthen bonds within the school community and provide a buffer against stressors that can lead to conflict.

6. Empowering Conflict Resolution Skills: Teaching students and staff practical conflict resolution skills—emphasizing active listening, empathy, and problem-solving—can help manage disagreements constructively, even in the face of stress and anxiety.

7. Adjusting Academic and Social Expectations: Recognizing when academic or social pressures become overwhelming and making adjustments can prevent stress and anxiety from escalating into conflicts. This may involve flexible deadlines, modified assignments, or additional support for students struggling to cope.

Stress and anxiety are significant drivers of conflict within educational settings, but their impact can be mitigated with the proper identification and management strategies. By fostering an environment that supports emotional well-being, promotes open communication, and provides the tools for stress management and constructive conflict resolution, schools can address the root causes of many conflicts. This proactive approach enhances the educational experience for all school community members and contributes to a culture of understanding, support, and resilience.

Navigating Cognitive Biases in Conflict Situations

Navigating cognitive biases in conflict situations is essential for understanding and resolving disputes effectively. Cognitive biases are mental shortcuts that our minds employ to form snap decisions about individuals and circumstances. However, they can also result in miscommunications, incorrect interpretations, and intensified disputes. People can become more adept at resolving conflicts and cultivating more objective, sympathetic, and productive relationships by becoming aware of and acting against these prejudices.

Understanding Cognitive Biases

Cognitive biases influence how we perceive and react to conflict. For example, confirmation bias leads us to pay more attention to information that supports our existing beliefs, while fundamental attribution error makes us more likely to blame others' negative actions on their character rather than external circumstances. These biases can skew our understanding of a conflict, leading to unfair judgments and preventing us from seeing the whole picture.

Strategies for Navigating Cognitive Biases

1. Awareness: The first step in navigating cognitive biases is becoming aware of them. Educating students, educators, and staff about common biases can help them recognize these patterns in their thinking.

2. Perspective-Taking: Trying to see the situation from the other person's point of view can counteract biases. This practice encourages empathy and can lead to a deeper understanding of the conflict's root causes.

3. Questioning Assumptions: Encourage individuals to question their initial assumptions about a conflict. Asking questions like "What evidence do I have for this belief?" or "Could there be another explanation?" can help challenge biased thinking.

4. Seeking Diverse Viewpoints: Exposure to different perspectives can help broaden understanding and counteract biases. This might involve discussing the conflict with a neutral third party or exploring the situation through role-play exercises in a school setting.

5. Focusing on Facts: Emphasizing the importance of factual information over opinions or assumptions can help mitigate the influence of biases. Encourage individuals to gather and share concrete evidence related to the conflict.

6. Reflective Practices: Implementing reflective practices, such as journaling or debriefing sessions after a conflict has been resolved, can help individuals recognize their biases and learn from them for future situations.

7. Mindfulness and Emotional Regulation: Mindfulness exercises and emotional regulation strategies can help individuals remain calm and objective in conflict situations, reducing the likelihood of biases clouding their judgment.

8. Continuous Learning and Development: An atmosphere more resilient to the negative impacts of cognitive biases can be created by promoting a culture of continuous learning in which people are willing to question their preconceptions and beliefs.

The Role of Educators and Institutions

Educators and school institutions play a crucial role in helping students navigate cognitive biases. This can be achieved through curriculum design that includes critical thinking and emotional intelligence, professional development focused on bias recognition and management for educators, and establishing school-wide initiatives that promote diversity, equity, and inclusion.

By equipping students and staff with the tools to recognize and address their cognitive biases, educational settings can become more conducive to constructive conflict resolution. This approach not only aids in resolving immediate disputes but also contributes to a more empathetic, understanding, and cohesive school community. Recognizing that biases are a natural part of human cognition, the goal is not to eliminate them but to understand their influence and mitigate their impact on conflict situations.

The Healing Power of Forgiveness in Resolving Conflicts

The healing power of forgiveness plays a crucial role in resolving conflicts, particularly within educational environments where positive relationships are foundational to learning and development. Forgiveness involves letting go of negative feelings like anger, resentment, or a desire for revenge against someone who has caused harm. Embracing forgiveness can lead to emotional healing, improved mental health, and more robust, positive relationships. Understanding and practicing forgiveness helps turn disagreements into chances for development and reconciliation in conflict resolution.

Forgiveness doesn't mean forgetting the harm done or excusing unacceptable behavior. Instead, it's about releasing past hurts' grip on our emotions and interactions, allowing individuals to move forward with a clearer perspective and a lighter heart. This shift benefits the person offering forgiveness and those who have caused harm, allowing them to acknowledge their actions, make amends, and work towards positive change.

Why Forgiveness Matters in Conflict Resolution

1. Reduces the Emotional Burden: Holding onto anger and resentment can be emotionally draining. Forgiveness helps lift this burden, leading to improved mental and emotional well-being.

2. Fosters Empathy and Understanding: Forgiving someone often requires understanding their actions from their perspective. This empathy may result in more understanding of the issue and the parties involved, opening the door to more successful solutions.

3. Strengthens Relationships: Conflicts can strain relationships, creating distance and mistrust. Forgiveness helps repair these rifts, rebuild trust, and reinforce the bonds between individuals.

4. Promotes a Positive School Culture: Encouraging forgiveness and modeling it within the school community can create a more supportive and respectful environment. This culture of forgiveness can reduce the frequency and intensity of conflicts.

5. Encourages Personal Growth: Forgiving can lead to personal growth and increased emotional intelligence. It teaches valuable lessons about compassion, understanding, and the complexity of human relationships.

Strategies for Encouraging Forgiveness

1. Facilitate Open Dialogue: Encourage open, honest communication about the conflict and the emotions it has stirred up. This dialogue should provide a safe space for expressing feelings, concerns, and needs.

2. Educate About Forgiveness: Integrate lessons on forgiveness into the curriculum or through special programs. Teach students about the benefits of forgiveness for themselves and their relationships.

3. Model Forgiveness: Educators and school staff should model forgiveness in their interactions. Demonstrating forgiveness in action can inspire students to embrace it in their own lives.

4. Support Emotional Expression and Processing: Help students express and process their emotions related to the conflict. This can involve counseling services, peer support groups, or creative arts therapies.

5. Highlight the Impact of Holding Grudges: Discuss the adverse effects of holding onto anger and resentment, not just on relationships but also on individual well-being.

6. Practice Empathy-Building Activities: Use role-playing, storytelling, or other activities to help students understand different perspectives and develop empathy, which is closely linked to forgiveness.

7. Encourage Restorative Practices: Implement restorative justice practices focusing on healing and making amends. These practices can facilitate forgiveness by addressing the harm done and working towards restitution.

Offering a way out of the vicious cycle of conflict and negativity, forgiveness is a potent instrument for healing and reconciliation. Schools may promote a culture of forgiveness to assist kids in learning how to manage their emotions constructively, strengthen relationships, and create a more positive, supportive learning environment. Embracing forgiveness does not negate the need for accountability or change but provides a foundation for meaningful resolution and growth.

Developing Resilience

Developing resilience is crucial for students and educators alike, as it equips them to navigate the challenges and setbacks they encounter both in and out of the classroom. Resilience, or the capacity to overcome adversity, promotes emotional fortitude, flexibility, and personal development. For students, resilience is critical to overcoming academic pressures, social challenges, and personal issues. For educators, it helps manage the demands of teaching and supporting students while maintaining their well-being. Here are strategies to build resilience in both students and educators.

Embrace a Growth Mindset

A growth mentality is predicated on the idea that talent and intelligence can be attained via perseverance and strenuous effort. This viewpoint enables teachers and students to see difficulties as chances to develop and learn rather than as insurmountable barriers. Encouraging this mindset can foster resilience by highlighting the value of effort, perseverance, and learning from mistakes.

Build Emotional Awareness

Understanding and managing emotions are critical components of resilience. Teaching students to recognize their feelings, understand why they feel that way, and how to express their emotions healthily can empower them to handle stress and setbacks more effectively. Educators should also practice emotional awareness, as it can help them respond to the demands of their role with greater clarity and calm.

Foster Strong Relationships

A supportive network of relationships is a cornerstone of resilience. Positive connections with peers, teachers, and family members can encourage and support students during tough times. Educators also benefit from strong professional networks and personal relationships that offer support, understanding, and a sense of belonging. Schools can foster these connections through team-building activities, mentoring programs, and creating a community-focused culture.

Teach Problem-Solving Skills

Equipping students and educators with problem-solving skills enables them to navigate challenges more effectively. This involves identifying problems, brainstorming, evaluating, and implementing solutions. Practicing these skills in various contexts helps develop a proactive approach to dealing with obstacles, enhancing resilience.

Encourage Self-Care

Sustaining one's physical, emotional, and mental well-being requires self-care. For students, this might include activities that promote relaxation, such as reading, sports, or creative arts. Educators should also prioritize self-care, ensuring they take time for activities that rejuvenate their energy and spirit. Schools can support self-care by creating a culture that values well-being and providing resources and time for self-care practices.

Promote Mindfulness and Stress Management Techniques

Mindfulness and stress management techniques can help students and educators manage stress and build resilience. Focus and emotional regulation can be improved, as can anxiety reduction through yoga, deep breathing, and meditation. Incorporating these practices into the school day or providing resources for students and staff to explore them independently can be beneficial.

Set Realistic Goals and Celebrate Achievements

Setting achievable goals and recognizing accomplishments can boost confidence and motivation, essential aspects of resilience. For students, goal-setting can focus on academic achievements, personal development, or extracurricular activities. Educators can set professional goals for teaching practices, student engagement, or personal growth. Celebrating these achievements, no matter how small, reinforces a sense of progress and capability.

Provide Resources and Support for Challenges

Schools should ensure that students and educators can access resources and support when facing challenges. This might include counseling services, academic support, professional development opportunities, and wellness programs. Knowing that support is available can make seeking help easier, an essential aspect of resilience.

Developing resilience is a dynamic process that benefits from a holistic approach, encompassing emotional intelligence, strong relationships, problem-solving skills, self-care, mindfulness, realistic goal-setting, and accessible support. By integrating these strategies into the educational experience, schools can nurture resilient students and educators prepared to face the challenges of today's world with strength, adaptability, and optimism.

The Psychology Behind Conflict Escalation and De-escalation

Understanding the psychology behind conflict escalation and de-escalation is crucial for effectively managing disputes, particularly in environments where maintaining harmony is essential, such as schools. Conflict escalation occurs when disagreements intensify in severity, often due to the actions and reactions of those involved, leading to a more complex situation to resolve. On the other hand, de-escalation involves strategies to reduce tension and resolve the dispute amicably. By exploring the psychological factors contributing to both processes, individuals can better navigate conflicts constructively.

Conflict Escalation: Understanding the Dynamics

1. Emotional Reactivity: One of the primary drivers of conflict escalation is emotional reactivity, where individuals respond to situations based on heightened emotions rather than rational thought. This can lead to actions that provoke further conflict instead of seeking resolution.

2. Miscommunication: Often, conflicts escalate because of misunderstandings or misinterpretations of someone's words or actions. Without clear communication, parties may assume harmful intentions, exacerbating the disagreement.

3. Confirmation Bias: Due to this bias, people tend to ignore evidence that contradicts their preexisting views or attitudes in favor of information that supports them. In conflicts, this can cause parties only to see proof that the other side is unreasonable or wrong, further entrenching their positions.

4. Fear of Losing Face: The desire to maintain one's image or not appear weak can drive individuals to escalate conflicts instead of conceding or compromising, fearing that doing so would undermine their authority or credibility.

De-escalation: Strategies for Calming Tensions

1. Active Listening: This involves genuinely listening to the other person's perspective without immediately responding. Active listening can validate the other party's feelings and open the door to understanding, reducing tensions.

2. Empathy: Trying to understand the situation from the other person's viewpoint can significantly de-escalate conflicts. Empathy facilitates a more compassionate approach to resolution, where solutions are sought that address the needs of all parties.

3. Clear and Respectful Communication: Communicating one's thoughts and feelings without blame or judgment can help prevent misinterpretations that might escalate the conflict. Respectful communication fosters a more constructive dialogue.

4. Managing Emotions: Individuals who regulate their emotional responses can better approach conflicts calmly and rationally. Techniques such as taking deep breaths, pausing before responding, or temporarily stepping away from the situation can help manage emotions effectively.

5. Seeking Common Ground: Identifying areas of agreement, even if they seem minor, can serve as a foundation for resolving broader disagreements. This approach shifts the focus from winning the argument to finding a mutually acceptable solution.

6. Using Neutral Mediators: In some cases, involving a neutral third party can help de-escalate conflicts. Mediators can offer a fresh perspective, facilitate fair communication, and suggest compromises the parties involved might not have considered.

The Role of Educators and School Administrators

Educators and administrators are pivotal in managing conflict escalation and de-escalation within schools. Modeling effective communication, emotional regulation, and conflict resolution strategies can create a positive environment that encourages students to manage disagreements constructively. Additionally, implementing programs that teach students about the psychology of conflicts and providing training in de-escalation techniques can equip the school community with the tools needed to navigate disputes effectively.

Understanding the psychological dynamics behind conflict escalation and de-escalation is essential for preventing disputes from spiraling out of control and resolving them in a way that promotes mutual respect and understanding. Individuals can more effectively manage conflicts by fostering active listening, empathy, clear communication, and being mindful of emotional reactivity and biases, contributing to a more harmonious and supportive educational environment.

Mindfulness and Conflict Resolution: Practical Applications

Practicing mindfulness, which is being fully present and engaged at the moment without passing judgment, offers several benefits for resolving conflicts. Individuals can improve their ability to navigate disagreements with calmness, empathy, and clarity by cultivating mindfulness. This approach can be particularly beneficial in educational settings, where conflicts can arise from the pressures and dynamics of the learning environment. Integrating mindfulness into conflict resolution processes can lead to more thoughtful interactions, better understanding, and constructive outcomes.

When practicing mindfulness amid conflict, the first step is to focus on one's breath. This simple act can help center the mind, reduce emotional reactivity, and provide the mental clarity needed to assess the situation objectively. By pausing and taking a few deep breaths, individuals can prevent immediate, often emotional, responses that might escalate the conflict. This pause creates space for a more considered approach to the disagreement.

Active listening is another area where mindfulness can have a profound impact. Giving the other person your whole attention while avoiding prejudging or formulating a reply is known as mindful listening. This form of listening can help uncover the underlying issues driving the conflict and demonstrate respect and care for the other person's perspective. When individuals feel heard and understood, it can significantly reduce tensions and open the path to resolution.

Mindfulness also enhances emotional regulation, a key component in managing conflicts effectively. Recognizing and accepting one's emotions without being overwhelmed allows for measured and constructive responses rather than reactive ones. This emotional awareness can also foster empathy, enabling individuals to appreciate the feelings and perspectives of those they are in conflict with, which is crucial for finding mutually acceptable solutions.

Practicing mindfulness can also involve reframing the conflict. Instead of viewing it as a battle to be won, mindfulness encourages seeing it as an opportunity for growth and learning. This shift in perspective can change the dynamic of the interaction, leading to more collaborative and creative problem-solving efforts.

Moreover, mindfulness encourages the acknowledgment of shared humanity. Recognizing that everyone has their struggles, fears, and vulnerabilities can foster a sense of connection and reduce the adversarial nature of conflicts. This acknowledgment can pave the way for compassion, understanding, and forgiveness.

Integrating mindfulness into conflict resolution can be achieved through various means in educational settings. Workshops and classes on mindfulness for students and educators can provide the tools and knowledge to apply mindfulness in everyday interactions. Creating quiet, reflective spaces within the school environment can also support mindfulness practices, offering places where individuals can calm their minds and emotions.

Furthermore, incorporating mindfulness exercises into the beginning of classes or meetings can set a tone of presence and attentiveness that benefits all forms of communication and interaction, including those involving conflict.

Mindfulness offers valuable tools for conflict resolution by promoting calmness, clarity, empathy, and a constructive approach to disagreements. By applying mindfulness practices to conflict situations, individuals can navigate disputes more effectively, leading to beneficial resolutions for all involved. In education, where positive relationships and a supportive environment are essential, mindfulness can be crucial in achieving these goals.

CHAPTER 9

INCLUSIVE EDUCATION AND CONFLICT RESOLUTION

C ultural competence in conflict resolution is increasingly recognized as essential in today's diverse educational environments. It refers to understanding, communicating, and effectively interacting with people across cultures. For educators, training in cultural competence can significantly improve how conflicts are managed and resolved in schools, ensuring that resolutions are respectful, equitable, and sensitive to the cultural backgrounds of all students.

Training programs for educators should focus on several key areas to enhance cultural competence in conflict resolution. The first area involves raising awareness of one's cultural background and biases. Everyone has biases, but awareness of them is the first step in ensuring they do not negatively influence conflict resolution processes. Educators can engage in self-reflection exercises, participate in workshops, and seek feedback from peers to become more aware of their biases and how they might impact their interactions with students and colleagues from different cultural backgrounds.

Another critical component is understanding the diverse student population's cultural norms, values, and communication styles. Cultures can vary significantly in how conflict is perceived and handled. For instance, some cultures might view confrontation as disrespectful, while others may see it necessary to resolve disagreements. Training programs should teach educators about different cultural frameworks and encourage them to consider these differences when managing conflicts. This could involve role-playing exercises, case studies, and interactions with cultural experts or members of different communities.

Effective communication strategies form another essential part of cultural competence training. Misunderstandings are a common source of conflict, exacerbating cultural differences in communication styles. Educators must learn to communicate clearly and sensitively across cultural divides, ensuring their language does not inadvertently offend or alienate students. This includes verbal communication and understanding non-verbal cues, which can vary significantly between cultures.

Developing empathy and an open-minded attitude is also crucial. Educators should be trained to approach conflicts with curiosity rather than judgment, seeking to understand the perspectives of all parties involved fully. This openness can help build trust with students and colleagues from diverse backgrounds and facilitate more effective conflict resolution.

Finally, training should include strategies for applying cultural competence in real-world conflict resolution scenarios. This might involve developing culturally sensitive policies and procedures for managing disputes, creating inclusive spaces where students feel safe expressing their concerns, and implementing restorative justice practices focusing on healing and community-building rather than punishment.

Incorporating cultural competence into conflict resolution training for educators enhances their ability to manage disputes effectively and contributes to a more inclusive, respectful, and supportive school environment. By understanding and appreciating their students' cultural backgrounds, educators can ensure that conflict resolution processes are fair, equitable, and conducive to the well-being and growth of all school community members.

Strategies for Addressing and Preventing Cultural and Racial Conflicts

Addressing and preventing cultural and racial conflicts requires a proactive and comprehensive approach, especially within educational environments where Diversity should be celebrated as a strength. These conflicts often stem from misunderstandings, biases, and systemic inequalities, making it crucial to develop strategies that resolve disputes when they arise and create a culture that minimizes the potential for such conflicts. Educators and students can work together to effectively address and prevent cultural and racial conflicts by fostering respect, inclusivity, and understanding.

Educational Programs on Cultural Awareness and Sensitivity

Implementing educational programs that focus on cultural awareness and sensitivity is fundamental. These programs should cover the history, traditions, and values of various cultures in the school community and racial discrimination's historical and systemic roots. By understanding these contexts, students and educators can become more empathetic and less likely to engage in behaviors that could lead to conflict.

Anti-bias Training

Anti-bias training for educators and staff is essential in creating an environment that actively counters prejudice and discrimination. This training should equip individuals with the skills to recognize their unconscious biases, understand how these biases can influence interactions and decisions, and implement strategies to mitigate their impact. Anti-bias training can also cover how to intervene effectively when witnessing prejudice or discrimination.

Inclusive Curriculum Development

Developing an inclusive curriculum that reflects the Diversity of the school community and the broader world can promote understanding and respect among students. This includes incorporating literature, history, and examples from various cultures and ensuring that teaching materials avoid stereotypes or omissions that could contribute to cultural misunderstandings or racial biases.

Open Dialogue and Communication Channels

Creating open channels for dialogue about cultural and racial issues is crucial. This can entail having regular class discussions, assemblies, or seminars where teachers and students can freely address racial and cultural issues, ask questions, and share personal stories. Safe spaces where individuals feel heard and respected can foster a deeper understanding and prevent potential conflicts.

Conflict Resolution Training

Training students and educators in conflict resolution techniques emphasizing empathy, active listening, and problem-solving can equip them with the tools to address disputes constructively when they arise. This training can also include specific strategies for navigating cultural and racial dynamics in conflicts, ensuring that resolutions are sensitive to the needs and perspectives of all parties involved.

Mentoring and Peer Support Programs

Mentoring and peer support programs can provide students with role models and confidants who understand their cultural or racial backgrounds. These programs can help students navigate challenges related to their identities, reduce feelings of isolation, and build a supportive community network.

Policies and Procedures for Addressing discrimination

It is essential to have explicit policies and processes for reporting and handling instances of bias and discrimination. These policies should outline the steps the school will take to investigate and resolve such incidents and the consequences for those found to have engaged in discriminatory behavior. Transparency in these policies and procedures can reinforce the school's commitment to a safe and inclusive environment.

Community Engagement and Partnerships

Engaging with the broader community and forming partnerships with local organizations can enhance efforts to address and prevent cultural and racial conflicts. Community leaders, cultural organizations, and advocacy groups can provide resources, support, and perspectives that enrich the school's initiatives and foster a sense of belonging among students.

Addressing and preventing cultural and racial conflicts in educational settings involves a multifaceted approach that includes academic programs, anti-bias training, inclusive curriculum development, open dialogue, conflict resolution training, mentoring, transparent policies, and community engagement. By implementing these strategies, schools can cultivate an environment where differences are respected and valued, conflicts are resolved constructively, and all students have the opportunity to thrive.

Inclusivity in Conflict Resolution Practices

Inclusivity in conflict resolution practices is essential for creating a fair and supportive environment where every community member feels valued and understood. Ensuring that all voices are heard, especially those that might be marginalized or overlooked, is crucial for achieving genuinely equitable and sustainable resolutions. This approach recognizes the Diversity within any group and seeks to address each individual's unique needs and perspectives.

Establishing environments where people feel comfortable expressing their opinions and feelings is crucial to practicing inclusion in conflict resolution. This means actively encouraging participation from all parties involved in a conflict and paying particular attention to those who may feel hesitant to speak up. Techniques such as round-robin sharing, where each person has a turn to speak without interruption, can ensure that everyone has the opportunity to be heard.

Understanding and respecting cultural differences play a significant role in inclusive conflict resolution. Cultural backgrounds can influence how individuals perceive conflict and how they prefer to resolve it. Being culturally sensitive and open to different conflict resolution styles can help bridge gaps in understanding and lead to more effective solutions. Training in cultural competence can equip participants with the knowledge and skills to navigate these differences respectfully.

Active listening is another critical component of inclusivity. To do this, listening must be done to understand rather than reacting or passing judgment. By practicing active listening, conflict resolution facilitators can create an atmosphere of empathy and respect where participants feel their perspectives are valued. Highlighting underlying issues that may not be immediately apparent can help clarify the debate.

Empowering underrepresented voices is crucial for inclusivity. This might involve providing additional support or resources for individuals less likely to speak up due to cultural, linguistic, or personal barriers. Facilitators can amplify these voices, ensuring their input is given equal weight in the resolution process.

Involving neutral third parties or mediators can also enhance inclusivity. A neutral mediator can help balance power dynamics within the conflict resolution, ensuring no single party dominates the conversation. This can be particularly important in situations where there are significant disparities in power or influence between the parties involved.

Flexibility in conflict resolution approaches allows for accommodating diverse needs and preferences. Recognizing that there is no one-size-fits-all solution to conflicts, inclusive practices are adaptable, drawing on various strategies and techniques to meet the specific circumstances of each case.

Feedback and follow-up are essential components of an inclusive conflict resolution process. After resolving, seeking feedback from all parties about the process and the outcome can provide valuable insights into its effectiveness and fairness. Follow-up meetings can guarantee that the resolution is being applied as intended and that all parties' demands are met.

Inclusivity in conflict resolution practices is more than just allowing everyone a chance to speak; it's about actively creating an environment where all perspectives are valued and considered. By prioritizing inclusivity, conflict resolution can lead to more just, effective, and lasting solutions, fostering a sense of belonging and respect within the community. Through understanding, active listening, empowering underrepresented voices, involving neutral mediators, being flexible, and providing feedback and follow-up, facilitators can ensure that all voices are heard and that resolutions reflect the diverse needs and experiences of those involved.

Gender Sensitivity in Conflict Management

Gender sensitivity in conflict management involves recognizing and addressing how individuals of various genders experience and engage in conflicts. It's about understanding the unique perspectives, needs, and challenges that gender can bring to conflict situations and ensuring that conflict management strategies are equitable and effective for everyone. Implementing gender-sensitive practices in conflict management is about fairness and enhancing the effectiveness of conflict resolution processes. Here are some best practices for incorporating gender sensitivity into conflict management.

Acknowledge and Understand Gender Dynamics

The first step is to recognize that gender dynamics can influence conflict situations. This includes understanding how societal norms and gender roles might impact individuals' behavior, communication styles, and comfort in expressing themselves in conflict situations. Educators and conflict resolution facilitators should be trained to recognize and consider these dynamics when managing conflicts.

Create Safe and Inclusive Spaces

Effective conflict resolution requires establishing a setting where people of all genders feel valued and comfortable. This may entail laying out precise rules for polite conduct and communication and ensuring everyone's physical and mental well-being comes first. Confidentiality and privacy should also be respected to encourage open and honest dialogue.

Use Gender-Inclusive Language

Using gender-inclusive language in all communications related to conflict management is essential for creating an environment of respect and inclusivity. This includes avoiding assumptions about individuals' gender identities based on their names or appearance and respecting individuals' preferred pronouns and terms of address.

Promote Equitable Participation

Ensure that individuals of all genders have equal opportunities to participate in the conflict resolution process. This might involve encouraging quieter or less confident individuals to share their perspectives and ensuring that no single voice dominates the conversation. Facilitators may need to employ strategies to balance power dynamics and ensure everyone's views are heard and valued.

Consider Gender-Specific Needs and Solutions

Recognize that individuals may have different needs and preferences for resolving conflicts based on gender. For example, some individuals may prefer private mediation over public discussion or require support services sensitive to gender-specific experiences. Being open to various conflict resolution strategies and tailoring approaches to meet these diverse needs can improve outcomes for all parties involved.

Provide Gender-Specific Support Services

Offering access to support services that are aware of and sensitive to gender-specific issues can be beneficial, especially in conflicts involving gender discrimination or harassment. This might include counseling services, legal advice, or support groups specializing in gender-related issues. Providing these resources demonstrates a commitment to addressing the root causes of conflicts and supporting all individuals involved.

Train Staff in Gender Sensitivity

Training for educators, administrators, and conflict resolution facilitators in gender sensitivity is essential. This training should cover the basics of gender dynamics, the impact of gender on conflict situations, and practical strategies for managing conflicts in a gender-sensitive manner. Training should address new issues related to gender identity and expression so that employees are prepared to manage various situations.

Monitor and Evaluate Conflict Resolution Processes

Regularly monitoring and evaluating conflict resolution processes can help identify whether they are effectively meeting the needs of individuals of all genders. This can involve collecting participant feedback about their experiences and adjusting practices based on this input. Continuous improvement ensures that conflict management strategies remain relevant and practical.

Integrating gender sensitivity into conflict management involves:

- Recognizing the impact of gender on conflict dynamics.
- Creating safe and inclusive environments.
- Using gender-inclusive language.
- Promoting equitable participation.
- Considering gender-specific needs.
- Providing appropriate support services.
- Training staff.
- Continuously monitoring and adjusting practices.

By implementing these best practices, schools and other organizations can ensure that conflict management processes are fair, respectful, and effective for individuals of all genders.

Addressing Conflicts in Special Education

Addressing conflicts in special education necessitates a nuanced and collaborative approach. Given students' unique needs and circumstances receiving special education services, disputes may arise from various sources, including disagreements over individualized education plans (IEPs), accommodations, or the

160

interpretation of educational rights. The goals of collaborative approaches to conflict resolution are:

- Open communication.
- Respect for one another.
- A shared commitment to the best interests of the student.

Fostering Open Communication

Open communication forms the bedrock of effective conflict resolution in special education. It involves creating an environment where parents, educators, and students feel comfortable expressing their concerns, needs, and preferences. Preventing misconceptions and addressing issues before they grow into more severe confrontations can be facilitated by holding regular meetings and updates, maintaining transparent and accessible communication channels, and making a commitment to listen without passing judgment.

Developing a Shared Understanding

Understanding the student's needs, strengths, and educational goals is crucial. This can be achieved through comprehensive assessments, transparent information sharing, and involving parents and students in the academic planning process as much as possible. Educators should ensure that all parties clearly understand special education laws, rights, and responsibilities, which can reduce conflicts arising from misinformation or misinterpretation.

Utilizing Collaborative IEP Meetings

IEP meetings are a central component of special education and should be approached with a collaborative mindset. Preparing for these meetings by setting clear agendas, inviting all relevant parties, and considering input from parents and students can facilitate a constructive dialogue. Utilizing facilitators or mediators during IEP meetings can also help manage discussions, especially when there are significant disagreements.

Implementing Conflict Resolution Teams

Conflict resolution teams comprising trained staff can provide an organized approach to resolving disputes. These teams can work with the involved parties to understand the conflict's root causes, explore solutions, and monitor the implementation of agreed-upon actions. Training for these teams should include specific strategies for navigating the complexities of notable education conflicts.

Promoting Mediation and Alternative Dispute Resolution

Mediation and other alternative dispute resolution (ADR) offer a confidential and non-adversarial way to address conflicts. These processes allow for exploring creative solutions that might not be available through formal dispute resolution mechanisms. Schools should provide information about available mediation services and encourage their use as a first step in resolving conflicts.

Encouraging Parent and Community Involvement

Parents and the wider community can be valuable allies in addressing and preventing conflicts. Schools can facilitate parent support groups, workshops, and information sessions to build a support community around special education issues. Engaging community resources, such as advocacy groups or legal assistance organizations, can provide additional support and guidance for families navigating conflicts.

Prioritizing Student Well-being and Inclusion

Ultimately, any conflict resolution effort in special education should focus on the student's well-being and inclusion. This means considering the student's voice and perspective in the resolution process and striving for solutions that respect the student's dignity, promote their development, and support their inclusion in the school community.

Monitoring and Reflecting on Outcomes

Regularly monitoring the outcomes of conflict resolution efforts and reflecting on their effectiveness is essential. This can involve gathering feedback from all parties involved, assessing the impact on the student's educational experience, and making adjustments as needed. Continuous improvement ensures that conflict resolution practices remain responsive to the needs of students receiving special education services.

Addressing conflicts in special education through collaborative approaches requires open communication, a shared understanding of the student's needs, the effective use of IEP meetings, conflict resolution teams, mediation and ADR, community involvement, and a steadfast commitment to student well-being and inclusion. By adopting these strategies, schools can create a supportive and constructive environment for resolving disputes, ultimately enhancing the educational experience for students receiving special education services.

Leveraging Diversity

Leveraging Diversity and turning conflicts into learning opportunities represent a transformative approach in educational settings. Conflicts arising from differences in cultural backgrounds, beliefs, and values are not merely challenges to be overcome; they are also valuable chances for growth, understanding, and enriching the school community. This perspective shifts the focus from conflict resolution to conflict transformation, where the goal is not only to resolve disagreements but also to use them as catalysts for learning and positive change.

163

Embrace Diversity as a Strength

The first step in leveraging Diversity is recognizing it as an invaluable asset to the learning environment. Diverse perspectives, experiences, and skills enhance creativity, problem-solving, and decision-making. Educators can highlight the benefits of Diversity by incorporating multicultural content into the curriculum, celebrating different cultures and traditions, and encouraging students to share their backgrounds and experiences.

Promote an Inclusive School Culture

Confrontations must be transformed into teaching moments by fostering an inclusive environment where all students are treated respectfully and feel important. This involves actively combating stereotypes, prejudice, and discrimination through education, policies, and practices that foster equity and respect. Encouraging open dialogue about Diversity and inclusion can help address biases and misunderstandings that often underlie conflicts.

Use Conflicts as Teachable Moments

When conflicts arise from Diversity, educators have a unique opportunity to use them as teachable moments. This can involve facilitating discussions that explore the roots of the conflict, the perspectives of all parties involved, and the broader societal context. These discussions help students develop critical thinking, empathy, and the ability to engage constructively with differing viewpoints.

Develop Conflict Resolution Skills

Equipping students with conflict resolution skills is crucial for transforming conflicts into opportunities for learning. This includes teaching strategies for active listening, expressing feelings and needs constructively, and seeking win-win solutions. Role-playing exercises and simulations can provide hands-on practice in navigating conflicts, preparing students to handle future disagreements more effectively.

Encourage Collaboration and Teamwork

Collaborative projects that bring together students from diverse backgrounds can foster mutual understanding and respect. By working towards a common goal, students can learn to appreciate each other's strengths, communicate effectively across differences, and build relationships that transcend cultural divides. These experiences can turn potential conflicts into opportunities for collective achievement.

Integrate Perspectives and Knowledge

Incorporating diverse perspectives and knowledge into teaching materials and classroom discussions can help students appreciate the value of different viewpoints. This approach enriches the learning experience and prepares students to navigate the diverse world beyond the classroom. By understanding multiple perspectives, students can better appreciate the complexity of conflicts and the importance of finding inclusive solutions.

Reflect on and Share Learning

After navigating a conflict, reflecting on the process and outcomes can consolidate learning. Students and educators can discuss what worked, what didn't, and how the experience contributed to their understanding of Diversity and conflict resolution. Sharing these reflections with the broader school community can amplify the learning benefits and encourage a culture of continuous improvement.

Celebrate Successes

Recognizing and celebrating successes in turning conflicts into learning opportunities can reinforce the positive aspects of Diversity. Whether it's a successfully resolved dispute, a collaborative project that bridged cultural divides, or an insightful classroom discussion, highlighting these achievements can motivate the school community to continue leveraging Diversity as a source of strength and learning.

Leveraging Diversity and turning conflicts into learning opportunities require a deliberate and thoughtful approach that values differences, promotes inclusion, and views challenges as chances for growth. By embracing Diversity, fostering an inclusive culture, using conflicts as teachable moments, and developing conflict resolution skills, educational settings can transform potential points of contention into rich learning experiences. This settles disputes immediately and gives pupils the information, abilities, and mindset they need to prosper in a multicultural society.

Community and School Partnerships for Inclusive Conflict Resolution

Community and school partnerships for inclusive conflict resolution embody a collaborative approach to managing disputes and fostering a positive school climate. Drawing on the strengths, perspectives, and resources of the school and the broader community, these partnerships can create more effective, culturally sensitive, and sustainable conflict resolution strategies. These collaborations can enrich the learning environment, provide additional support for students and educators, and ensure that conflict resolution practices are inclusive and reflective of the community's Diversity.

Building a Foundation for Partnership

Mutual respect, trust, and common objectives are the cornerstones of a thriving community and school cooperation. Establishing clear communication channels, defining roles and responsibilities, and creating regular feedback and adjustment mechanisms can solidify this foundation. Both schools and community organizations should commit to ongoing dialogue to understand each other's strengths, challenges, and expectations.

Leveraging Community Resources

Communities are rich in resources that can enhance conflict resolution efforts in schools. These include local mediation services, cultural organizations, youth programs, and mental health providers. By tapping into these resources, schools can offer a broader range of conflict resolution options tailored to their students' needs. For example, community mediators can bring a neutral perspective to school disputes, while cultural organizations can provide insights and training on managing conflicts that arise from cultural differences.

Cultural Competence and Sensitivity

One key benefit of community and school partnerships is the opportunity to enhance cultural competence and sensitivity in conflict resolution practices. Community organizations, especially those focused on serving specific cultural or demographic groups, can offer valuable training and guidance for educators. This can help ensure that conflict resolution strategies are respectful and effective for the diverse student population.

Joint Training and Professional Development

Joint training sessions and professional development opportunities for educators and community partners can foster a cohesive approach to conflict resolution. These sessions can cover various topics, from basic mediation techniques and active listening skills to more specialized training on addressing biases, navigating cultural differences, and supporting students with special needs. Shared learning experiences can also strengthen the bonds between school staff and community members, enhancing their ability to work together effectively.

Involving Students and Families

Students and families should actively participate in community and school partnerships for inclusive conflict resolution. Engaging students in leadership roles like peer mediation programs can empower them to contribute to a positive school climate. Similarly, involving families in conflict resolution processes and decision-making ensures that their perspectives and needs are considered. This inclusive approach can build trust, encourage collaboration, and ensure that conflict resolution strategies are grounded in the realities of students' lives.

Evaluating and Celebrating successes

Regular evaluation of the partnership's impact on conflict resolution outcomes is essential for continuous improvement. Both schools and community partners should establish metrics for success, collect data on conflict resolution processes and outcomes, and adjust strategies based on this feedback. Celebrating successes through public recognition, events, or communications can highlight the partnership's value and motivate ongoing collaboration.

Sustaining the Partnership

Sustaining community and school partnerships over the long term requires commitment, flexibility, and recognition of the evolving needs of the school and the community. Securing funding, whether through grants, donations, or school budgets, can support the continuation of joint programs and initiatives. Equally important is nurturing the relationship between the school and community partners, ensuring that it remains strong even as personnel and circumstances change.

Community and school partnerships for inclusive conflict resolution offer a powerful approach to managing disputes, enhancing educational outcomes, and fostering a school climate that values Diversity, respect, and cooperation. By leveraging the strengths and resources of both the school and the broader community, these partnerships can create conflict resolution strategies that are more effective, culturally sensitive, and sustainable, ultimately contributing to the well-being and success of all students.

CHAPTER 10

LEADERSHIP AND CONFLICT MANAGEMENT

The atmosphere around school conflict is greatly influenced by the leadership styles employed. How school leaders, including principals, department heads, and senior teachers, handle disputes and model conflict resolution can significantly affect how staff and students perceive and engage with disputes. Leadership styles vary widely, each with a unique impact on the school's approach to managing disagreements, fostering a communication culture, and ultimately determining its overall conflict climate.

Authoritative Leadership

Authoritative leaders are characterized by their clear vision and firm but fair approach. They set high expectations and guide their staff and students toward achieving these goals with a supportive attitude. Regarding conflict, authoritative leaders seek constructive solutions that respect the needs and opinions of all parties involved. Their approach to conflict resolution can foster a positive climate by promoting open communication, mutual respect, and collaborative problem-solving. Students and staff feel valued and heard, creating a more harmonious and cooperative school environment.

Autocratic Leadership

Autocratic leaders tend to make decisions unilaterally, with little input from others. In conflict situations, this top-down approach can suppress open discussion and may lead to resolutions that favor the leader's perspective, potentially overlooking the needs of other parties. Although this approach could settle conflicts quickly, it can foster animosity and disengagement. Over time, this can stifle open communication and discourage individuals from voicing concerns or disagreements, leading to unresolved issues simmering beneath the surface.

Democratic Leadership

Democratic leaders prioritize participation and collaboration. They involve staff and students in decision-making processes, including conflict resolution. This inclusive approach encourages diverse viewpoints and democratic deliberation to find mutually acceptable solutions. The impact on the school's conflict climate is generally positive, as individuals feel empowered and respected. This style fosters a culture of Transparency and trust, where conflicts are seen as opportunities for dialogue and growth rather than obstacles to be avoided.

Laissez-faire Leadership

Laissez-faire leaders take a hands-off approach, allowing staff and students significant autonomy in managing conflicts. While this can promote independence and self-reliance, it might also lead to inconsistencies in conflict resolution and a lack of support for those who struggle to navigate disputes independently. The impact on the school's conflict climate can be mixed; while some may thrive under the freedom to solve their problems, others may feel neglected or overwhelmed, potentially exacerbating conflicts.

Transformational Leadership

Transformational leaders aim to inspire and motivate, focusing on shared values and goals to elevate the school community. They are characterized by their ability to foster strong relationships and encourage personal and collective growth. Transformational leaders seek to identify the underlying causes of conflicts and find solutions supporting the school's goals. This approach can positively impact the school's conflict climate by promoting unity and purpose, encouraging constructive conflict resolution, and modeling positive behaviors.

Servant Leadership

Servant leaders put the needs of others above their own, emphasizing the uplift and empowerment of individuals under their direction. In conflicts, servant leaders are attentive to the needs and perspectives of all involved, striving for resolutions that serve the greater good. This leadership style can significantly enhance the school's conflict climate by creating an environment where empathy, service, and mutual support are valued. It encourages a community-oriented approach to conflict resolution, focusing on healing and building stronger relationships.

The leadership style of school administrators and senior staff members significantly influences the school's conflict climate. Authoritative, democratic, transformational, and servant leadership styles promote a more positive conflict climate characterized by open communication, mutual respect, and collaborative problem-solving. In contrast, autocratic and laissez-faire leadership styles lead to a less favorable conflict climate, where issues may be suppressed or unresolved. Recognizing the impact of leadership on conflict dynamics is crucial for fostering a supportive and constructive environment within schools.

Empowering Student Leadership in Conflict Resolution

Empowering student leadership in conflict resolution transforms how schools approach disputes, creating a culture where students are part of the solution. This methodology endows pupils with fundamental life competencies and cultivates a feeling of accountability and proprietorship toward establishing a peaceful educational setting. Schools can benefit from innovative perspectives and solutions directly relevant to the student body by involving students in conflict resolution.

Student Mediation Programs

One effective way to empower student leadership in conflict resolution is through student mediation programs. These programs train students to serve as mediators in disputes among their peers. Student mediators learn to facilitate discussions, help parties understand each other's perspectives, and guide them toward mutually agreeable solutions. This peer-led approach can be efficient as students often feel more comfortable discussing issues with their peers than with adults. Additionally, seeing conflicts resolved by fellow students reinforces that constructive resolution is achievable and desirable.

Conflict Resolution Workshops and Training

Offering workshops and training sessions on conflict resolution equips students with the knowledge and skills to handle disagreements constructively. These sessions can cover active listening, empathy, negotiation, and problem-solving topics. By incorporating these workshops into the school curriculum or as extracurricular activities, schools can ensure that all students have access to this valuable learning opportunity. Students who perform well in these workshops may also be encouraged to assume leadership positions in conflict resolution councils or peer mediation programs.

Student Conflict Resolution Councils

Creating student conflict resolution councils is another strategy for empowering student leadership. These councils, composed of students from different grades and backgrounds, can work alongside school administrators to develop policies, organize training sessions, and spearhead initiatives that promote a positive school climate. Council members can also serve as ambassadors of conflict resolution, modeling constructive behavior and supporting their peers.

Incorporating Technology

Leveraging Technology can enhance student leadership in conflict resolution. Social media and online platforms can be used to set up forums where students can discuss and resolve problems anonymously, exchange resources, and arrange virtual mediation sessions. Apps and websites for conflict resolution can also provide students with tools to manage disputes independently, encouraging proactive and positive engagement with conflicts.

Service Learning and Community Projects

Service learning and community projects focusing on conflict resolution and peace-building can offer practical experiences reinforcing the principles learned in workshops and training. Students can apply their skills meaningfully by participating in projects that address real-world conflicts in their school or the broader community. These experiences contribute to personal and academic growth and demonstrate constructive conflict resolution's impact on community well-being.

Mentorship Programs

Mentorship programs that pair younger students with older students experienced in conflict resolution can facilitate the transfer of knowledge and skills. Mentors can provide guidance, support, and practical advice to mentees, helping them navigate conflicts effectively. This one-on-one approach can be especially beneficial for students struggling with conflicts, offering them personalized support and a positive role model.

Celebrating Successes

Recognizing and celebrating the successes of student leaders in conflict resolution is crucial for sustaining their engagement and motivation. There are many other ways to celebrate, such as giving out trophies and certificates or publicly praising someone in newsletters or school assemblies. Highlighting the achievements of student mediators, council members, and other leaders not only honors their contributions but inspires other students to get involved.

Empowering student leadership in conflict resolution enriches the educational experience by promoting skills essential for personal and academic success. It fosters a culture in the classroom where disagreements are seen as learning opportunities rather than roadblocks and where students actively contribute to fostering a welcoming and happy environment. Through mediation programs, workshops, councils, Technology, service projects, mentorship, and celebration of successes, schools can harness the power of student leadership to foster a more harmonious and supportive community.

Collaborative Leadership

Collaborative leadership in conflict management is a powerful approach that involves engaging staff at all levels in addressing and resolving disputes within the school environment. Transparency, group accountability, and shared decision-making are the hallmarks of this leadership approach. By integrating staff in conflict management, leaders can use various viewpoints and experiences, resulting in more durable and practical solutions. Here's how collaborative leadership can be implemented to engage staff in conflict management processes.

Fostering an Open Communication Culture

Creating a culture of open communication is the first step in engaging staff in conflict management. This entails motivating employees to voice their ideas, worries, and proposals without holding back for fear of negative consequences. Regular staff meetings, suggestion boxes, and open-door policies facilitate this exchange of ideas. Transparency about conflict management processes and decisions reinforces this culture, as staff feel respected and valued when informed.

Providing Training and Development

Providing employees with the abilities and information needed to resolve disputes amicably is essential. Training programs focusing on communication skills, emotional intelligence, and conflict resolution approaches can help achieve this. Professional development opportunities can also aid employees in developing a deeper comprehension of the underlying factors that lead to conflicts, such as organizational dynamics or cultural differences. By investing in staff training, leaders demonstrate their commitment to a collaborative approach to conflict management.

Creating Conflict Resolution Teams

Forming conflict resolution teams composed of staff members from various departments and roles can promote a collaborative approach to managing disputes. These teams can assess conflicts, facilitate mediation sessions, and develop intervention strategies. Involving staff in these teams leverages their expertise and fosters a sense of ownership over the conflict-resolution process.

Implementing Shared Decision-Making

Collaborative leadership involves sharing decision-making responsibilities with staff, especially when developing conflict management policies and procedures. This could include forming committees to review and update conflict management policies or involving staff in developing new initiatives. Shared decision-making ensures that policies and procedures are grounded in the realities of the school environment and have the support of the entire staff.

Encouraging Peer Support and Mediation

Peer support and mediation programs can empower staff to support each other in managing conflicts. Training staff as peer mediators can provide an internal resource for resolving disputes before they escalate. Peer support networks can also offer emotional and practical support to staff navigating challenging situations. These programs promote a collaborative spirit, with staff members helping each other to maintain a positive and productive work environment.

Seeking Feedback and Reflecting on Practices

Regularly seeking feedback from staff on the effectiveness of conflict management strategies is essential for continuous improvement. Surveys, focus groups, and feedback sessions can all provide enlightening details on what is and is not working. Reflecting on this feedback and making necessary changes demonstrates a commitment to a collaborative and responsive approach to conflict management.

Celebrating Successes Together

Recognizing and celebrating successes in conflict resolution reinforces the value of a collaborative approach. This could include acknowledging the contributions of conflict resolution teams, sharing stories of successful conflict management, or celebrating the resolution of a particularly challenging dispute. Celebrations can boost morale and motivate staff to continue engaging in collaborative conflict management efforts.

Collaborative leadership in conflict management recognizes that effective solutions to disputes often require the collective efforts of the entire staff. By fostering open communication, providing training, creating conflict resolution teams, implementing shared decision-making, encouraging peer support, seeking feedback, and celebrating successes, leaders can engage staff in creating a more harmonious and supportive school environment. This approach not only enhances the resolution of current conflicts but also builds the school community's capacity to manage future disputes constructively.

Ethical Leadership in Navigating School Conflicts

Ethical leadership in navigating school conflicts emphasizes the importance of integrity, fairness, and respect in the resolution process. Ethical leaders act as role models, demonstrating how to handle disagreements constructively while upholding the values and principles of the school community. This approach to leadership ensures that conflict resolution not only addresses the immediate issue but also reinforces the moral framework within which the school operates. Here's how ethical leadership can guide the management of school conflicts.

Modeling Ethical Behavior

Ethical leaders exemplify the behavior they expect from others. This means approaching disputes honestly and open-mindedly and a commitment to fairness in conflict situations. By modeling respectful communication and showing empathy for all parties involved, leaders set a standard for managing conflicts throughout the school. This ethical behavior model promotes a culture in which people are more inclined to participate in positive conflict resolution processes because they feel comfortable and supported in voicing their opinions.

Ensuring Fairness and Impartiality

One of the hallmarks of ethical leadership is the commitment to fairness and impartiality in conflict resolution. Ethical leaders strive to understand all sides of a conflict without prejudice, ensuring everyone's voice is heard and considered. Decisions are made based on a balanced assessment of the situation rather than personal biases or relationships. This fairness not only aids in finding equitable solutions but also builds trust in the leadership and the conflict resolution process.

Promoting Transparency

Transparency is critical to ethical leadership, especially in the context of conflicts. Leaders should communicate openly about how disputes are handled, the steps in the resolution process, and the rationale behind the decisions. This Transparency helps demystify the conflict resolution process, reducing rumors and misunderstandings that can exacerbate tensions. It also reinforces leadership's accountability to the school community.

Prioritizing the Well-being of All Involved

Ethical leaders prioritize the emotional and physical well-being of everyone involved in a conflict. This means providing support services, such as counseling or mediation, and ensuring the resolution process does not exacerbate stress or harm. Recognizing the human element in conflicts and protecting individuals' well-being demonstrates a compassionate and ethical approach to leadership.

Fostering a Culture of Ethical Decision-Making

Beyond individual conflicts, ethical leaders work to foster a school-wide culture that values ethical decision-making. This can involve integrating ethics into the curriculum, training staff and students on ethical reasoning, and creating forums for discussion about moral dilemmas and values. By cultivating an environment where ethical considerations are part of everyday decision-making, leaders can help prevent conflicts that arise from unethical behavior.

Encouraging Restorative Practices

Restorative practices align closely with ethical leadership by focusing on healing and making amends rather than punishment. Ethical leaders encourage approaches that seek to understand the impact of conflicts, restore relationships, and reintegrate individuals into the community. This emphasis on restoration over retribution reflects a commitment to forgiveness, compassion, and growth.

Reflecting and Learning from Conflicts

Finally, ethical leadership involves reflecting on how conflicts are managed and what can be learned. This reflection considers the outcomes and whether the process aligned with the school's values and ethical standards. Leaders should be receptive to criticism and flexible to better align their actions with ethical standards. Learning from conflicts ensures continuous improvement and reinforces the importance of ethics in shaping the school community.

Ethical leadership provides a foundation for navigating school conflicts in a way that respects the dignity of all parties, upholds justice, and reinforces the school community's values. By modeling ethical behavior, ensuring fairness, promoting Transparency, prioritizing well-being, fostering a culture of ethical decision-making, encouraging restorative practices, and reflecting on and learning from each situation, leaders can navigate school conflicts in a way that strengthens the school's moral fabric and supports a positive and respectful learning environment.

Leadership Training for Effective Conflict Resolution

Leadership training for effective conflict resolution equips current and aspiring leaders with the skills and insights necessary to manage disputes constructively within their organizations or communities. This training focuses on developing comprehensive competencies, including communication, empathy, negotiation, and problem-solving skills. By empowering leaders with these tools, organizations can foster a more harmonious environment, enhance collaboration, and ensure that conflicts lead to positive outcomes rather than disruption.

Core Components of Leadership Training for Conflict Resolution

1. Understanding Conflict Dynamics: Training begins with exploring the nature of conflict, including its causes, types, and stages. Leaders learn to recognize early signs of conflict and understand the underlying issues that may not be immediately apparent. This foundation is critical for preemptively addressing tensions before they escalate.

2. Communication Skills: Effective communication is the key to resolving conflicts. Leaders are trained in active listening techniques, assertive communication, and expressing thoughts and feelings clearly, respectfully, and in a manner conducive to dialogue. Emphasis is placed on language's power to escalate or de-escalate situations.

3. Emotional Intelligence: Leaders are taught to manage their emotions and recognize the emotional states of others. Training in emotional intelligence includes developing empathy, self-regulation, and maintaining composure under pressure. These skills are essential for navigating emotionally charged conflict situations with sensitivity and care.

4. Negotiation and Mediation Skills: Participants learn negotiation techniques to find mutually beneficial solutions. Training may also cover mediation skills, enabling leaders to act as neutral third parties to facilitate discussions between conflicting parties and guide them toward resolution.

5. Problem-solving Strategies: Leaders are equipped with various problem-solving frameworks and strategies that encourage creative thinking and collaborative solution-finding. These consist of methods for generating ideas, weighing possibilities, and implementing fixes that deal with the underlying causes of disputes.

6. Cultural Competence: Recognizing and respecting diversity is crucial in conflict resolution. Leaders receive training on cultural awareness and sensitivity, learning to navigate conflicts that may arise from cultural misunderstandings or biases, and ensuring that resolution strategies are inclusive and equitable.

7. Ethical Decision-Making: Ethical considerations are central to conflict resolution. Training emphasizes the importance of fairness, integrity, and respect for all parties involved. Leaders learn to make decisions that align with organizational values and ethical standards.

8. Personal Reflection and Self-Care: Leaders are encouraged to reflect on their conflict resolution style, including their strengths and areas for improvement. Training also highlights the importance of self-care, recognizing that managing conflicts can be emotionally taxing and that leaders must take care of their well-being to remain effective.

Implementing Leadership Training for Conflict Resolution

Organizations can implement leadership training for conflict resolution in various formats, including workshops, seminars, online courses, and coaching sessions. Tailoring the training to the organization's specific context and needs can enhance its relevance and effectiveness. Ongoing support, such as follow-up sessions, peer learning groups, and access to conflict resolution resources, can help leaders continue to develop their skills over time.

Real-world case studies and role-playing activities can help leaders implement what they have learned in a safe and encouraging setting by giving them real-world experience. Additionally, involving experienced conflict resolution practitioners as trainers or mentors can offer valuable insights and guidance.

Leadership training for effective conflict resolution is a comprehensive program that builds essential skills for managing disputes constructively. By focusing on communication, emotional intelligence, negotiation, problem-solving, cultural competence, and ethical decision-making, organizations can prepare their leaders to handle conflicts to promote understanding, collaboration, and positive change. This investment in leadership development benefits the leaders themselves and contributes to the organization's overall health and success.

Role of School Leaders in Mediating Complex Conflicts

The pivotal role of school leaders in mediating complex conflicts is that they are not just administrators but also key facilitators of peace and understanding within the educational environment. Complex school conflicts arise from various sources, including interpersonal disputes, cultural misunderstandings, or school policy and practice issues. Effective mediation by school leaders can transform these conflicts into opportunities for growth, learning, and community strengthening.

Understanding the Nature of Conflicts

School leaders must first understand the nature and root causes of conflicts. Complex conflicts often have multiple layers, involving immediate disagreement and underlying issues such as power imbalances, historical grievances, or emotional trauma. Leaders must approach these situations with a deep understanding and sensitivity to navigate the intricacies involved effectively.

Creating a Safe and Respectful Environment

Mediation requires a safe and respectful environment where all parties feel heard and valued. School leaders can foster this environment by establishing clear guidelines for respectful communication and demonstrating the importance of empathy and understanding through their actions. This safe space encourages open dialogue, allowing all sides of the conflict to be explored without fear of judgment or retaliation.

Active Listening and Impartiality

One critical role of school leaders in mediation is to practice active listening. This involves giving full attention to the speakers, understanding their messages, and acknowledging their feelings. Leaders must remain impartial, ensuring their biases or preconceptions do not influence the mediation process. This impartiality helps build trust and facilitate a more productive dialogue.

Facilitating Constructive Dialogue

Leaders must guide the conversation in a way that promotes understanding and collaboration. This might involve helping parties articulate their feelings and needs, asking open-ended questions to explore the issues more deeply, and identifying common ground. The goal is to move from confrontation to collaboration, where parties work together to find mutually satisfactory solutions.

Empowering Parties to Find Solutions

Effective mediation empowers the conflicting parties to take an active role in resolving the dispute. School leaders can facilitate this by encouraging participants to suggest solutions and explore their consequences. This empowerment fosters a sense of ownership over the resolution process and increases the likelihood of a lasting agreement.

Providing Resources and Support

Complex conflicts may require resources and support beyond the mediation session. School leaders can connect parties with counseling services, academic support, or other resources to address underlying issues contributing to the conflict. Additionally, follow-up meetings can ensure that the agreed-upon solutions are implemented and that parties continue to build a positive relationship.

Modeling and Teaching Conflict Resolution Skills

School leaders play a crucial role in modeling conflict resolution skills for students and staff. Leaders demonstrate effective strategies that others can emulate by handling conflicts with grace, patience, and fairness. Furthermore, incorporating conflict resolution education into the school curriculum can equip the school community with the skills to handle disagreements constructively.

Reflecting and Learning from Each Conflict

Finally, school leaders should reflect on each conflict and the mediation process to learn from the experience. This reflection can inform future approaches to conflict resolution, helping leaders refine their strategies and better serve their school communities. Providing workers access to these reflections and lessons gained can also foster a culture of ongoing development and cooperative problem-solving.

School leaders' role in mediating complex conflicts is multifaceted and crucial for maintaining a positive school climate. By understanding the nature of conflicts, creating a safe environment, practicing active listening, facilitating constructive dialogue, empowering parties to find solutions, providing necessary resources, modeling conflict resolution skills, and reflecting on each experience, school leaders can effectively mediate disputes and foster a culture of understanding and respect within the school community.

Creating a Vision for a Conflict-Resilient School Community

Creating a vision for a conflict-resilient school community involves imagining an educational environment where conflicts are not feared but are seen as opportunities for growth, learning, and strengthening relationships. In a conflict-resilient school, students, educators, and staff possess the skills and mindset to navigate disagreements constructively, and the school's culture and policies support these positive interactions. Achieving this vision requires a comprehensive and proactive approach, emphasizing communication, education, inclusivity, and community engagement.

Fostering a Culture of Open Communication

A conflict-resilient school prioritizes open, honest communication. This means creating multiple channels for students, staff, and parents to express concerns, share ideas, and provide feedback. Regular meetings, suggestion boxes, and digital platforms can facilitate this communication. Promoting open communication and active listening among all individuals fosters trust and averts misconceptions that may result in disputes.

Educating the Community on Conflict Resolution

Investing in conflict resolution education for the entire school community is crucial. Workshops, seminars, and classes can teach students and staff effective strategies for managing disagreements, such as active listening, empathy, negotiation, and mediation. Embedding these lessons into the curriculum ensures that conflict resolution becomes a foundational skill learned alongside academic subjects.

Promoting Emotional Intelligence

Emotional intelligence—the ability to understand and manage one's emotions and to empathize with others—is critical to navigating conflicts constructively. Programs that develop emotional intelligence help individuals respond to disagreements with calmness and clarity, fostering a more harmonious school environment.

Building Inclusive Policies and Practices

Inclusivity is at the heart of a conflict-resilient school. Policies and practices should reflect the diversity of the school community, ensuring that all voices are heard and valued. This inclusivity extends to conflict resolution processes, where diverse perspectives are considered, and solutions that respect everyone's needs and rights are sought.

Implementing Restorative Practices

Restorative practices focus on healing and making amends rather than punishment. By adopting these practices, schools can resolve conflicts in a way that strengthens relationships and builds a sense of community. Restorative circles, peer mediation, and conflict resolution teams can be part of the school's dispute management approach.

Encouraging Leadership and Student Involvement

Leadership and student involvement are vital for creating a conflict-resilient school. Training students as peer mediators, involving them in conflict resolution councils, and encouraging them to take leadership roles in school initiatives empower them to contribute to a positive school climate. Educators and administrators should model constructive conflict resolution and support student efforts.

Engaging with the Wider Community

A conflict-resilient school is not isolated; it is part of the broader community. Engaging with parents, local organizations, and community leaders can bring additional resources, perspectives, and support to the school's conflict resolution efforts. Community partnerships can enrich the school's programs and extend the culture of conflict resilience beyond the school gates.

Continuously Evaluating and Improving

Creating a conflict-resilient school is an ongoing process. Regular evaluation of conflict resolution policies, practices, and outcomes is essential for understanding what works and needs adjustment. Soliciting feedback from the school community and being open to change ensures that the school's approach to conflict resolution remains effective and responsive to the community's needs.

Envisioning a conflict-resilient school community involves creating an environment where open communication, emotional intelligence, inclusivity, restorative practices, leadership, community engagement, and continuous improvement are valued and practiced. By committing to these principles, schools can transform how conflicts are perceived and handled, creating a more supportive, understanding, and resilient community.

CHAPTER 11

PARENTAL ENGAGEMENT IN CONFLICT RESOLUTION

Effective communication strategies between parents and schools are fundamental to fostering a supportive and collaborative educational environment for students. Clear, open, and consistent communication builds trust, ensures that both parties are informed about students' progress and well-being, and facilitates swift resolution of any issues that arise. Here's how schools can enhance communication with parents, thereby strengthening the home-school partnership.

Establish Clear Communication Channels

Schools should establish various communication channels to accommodate different preferences and needs. This might include email, phone calls, text messaging systems, school websites, and social media platforms. Furthermore, it is possible to guarantee that all parents have access to important information by providing a safe and secure web gateway via which they can learn about their child's academic achievement, attendance records, and school announcements.

Regular Updates and Newsletters

Regular updates can inform parents about school events, policy changes, and other important announcements through email newsletters, printed bulletins, or online posts. These updates should be concise, clear, and regular, ensuring that parents feel connected to the school community and know the opportunities to get involved.

Scheduled Conferences and Meetings

Parent-teacher conferences are:

- A cornerstone of effective communication.
- Providing an opportunity for in-depth discussions about students' academic performance.
- Behavior.
- Social development.

Schools might also consider offering virtual meeting options to increase accessibility for parents. Encouraging parents to prepare questions or concerns in advance can make these meetings more productive and focused.

Workshops and Information Sessions

Hosting workshops and information sessions on topics relevant to parents, such as curriculum overviews, college preparation, internet safety, or strategies for supporting learning at home, can be highly beneficial. These sessions provide valuable information and open up additional lines of communication between parents and the school.

Feedback Mechanisms

Creating mechanisms for parents to provide feedback to the school is crucial. This could be through surveys, suggestion boxes, or parent advisory committees. Actively seeking parents' input on school policies, programs, and practices demonstrates respect for their perspectives and contributes to community and collaboration.

Responsive Communication

Schools must ensure that communication is not just outgoing but also responsive. It is essential to establish a clear protocol for how and when parents can expect responses to their inquiries or concerns. This might include standard email response times, designated staff members to handle different types of inquiries, and regular office hours when parents can call or visit.

Cultural and Linguistic Consideration

Recognizing and accommodating the cultural and linguistic diversity of the school community is essential for effective communication. This might involve translating written communications, offering interpretation services during meetings and events, and ensuring that cultural differences are respected and reflected in the school's communication efforts.

Empowering Teachers and Staff

Training teachers and staff in effective communication techniques can empower them to engage more confidently and effectively with parents. This training might cover active listening, cultural competence, conflict resolution, and strategies for communicating sensitive issues.

Building Positive Relationships

Finally, the foundation of effective communication between parents and schools is cultivating positive, respectful relationships. By acknowledging and appreciating parents' contributions to the school community, giving parents the opportunity to participate in school events, and ensuring that all conversations are conducted with a tone of respect and understanding, schools may promote these connections.

Effective communication strategies between parents and schools are vital for supporting students' educational journeys. By establishing clear channels, providing regular updates, being responsive to parents' needs, and fostering positive relationships, schools can create a collaborative and supportive partnership with parents, enhancing the overall educational experience for students.

Parent Workshops on Conflict Management Skills

Parent workshops on conflict management skills are an invaluable resource in the educational community. They bridge the gap between home and school, empowering parents with practical tools for navigating conflicts. These workshops can provide parents with insights into conflict resolution strategies that benefit home and school settings, fostering a more harmonious environment for children's growth and development. Implementing such workshops requires thoughtful planning, focusing on relevant content, interactive learning experiences, and practical applications that parents can use daily.

Workshop Content

1. Understanding Conflict: Introduce the concept of Conflict as a natural part of human interactions, emphasizing that constructive conflict resolution can lead to personal growth and stronger relationships.

2. **Identifying Conflict Styles:** Explore different conflict styles and their impacts on conflict outcomes. Encourage parents to reflect on their conflict styles and how they affect their family dynamics.

3. **Active Listening and Communication Skills** : Instruct parents on the value of good communication and attentive listening

in dispute resolution. Include exercises that enhance listening skills, such as paraphrasing and asking open-ended questions.

4. Emotional Intelligence: This section covers the role of emotional intelligence in conflict resolution, including understanding one's emotions, empathizing with others, and managing emotional responses in high-tension situations.

5. Problem-Solving Strategies: Provide parents with strategies for collaborative problem-solving, including identifying the root cause of conflicts, brainstorming solutions, and agreeing on a course of action that meets everyone's needs.

6. Setting Boundaries and Expectations: Discuss the importance of setting clear boundaries and expectations within the family as a preventive measure against conflicts. Offer guidance on how to establish and communicate these boundaries respectfully and effectively.

Interactive Learning Experiences

1. Role-Playing Exercises: Create scenarios parents might encounter at home or in school-related situations. Allow parents to role-play these scenarios, practicing conflict resolution strategies in a supportive environment.

2. Group Discussions: Facilitate group discussions on common challenges parents face in managing conflicts. This encourages sharing experiences and strategies, fostering a sense of community and mutual support.

3. Skills Practice Sessions: Include hands-on sessions where parents can apply communication and problem-solving skills in simulated conflict situations.

Practical Applications

1. Home Conflict Resolution Plan: Guide parents in developing a personalized conflict resolution plan for their family, incorporating the strategies and skills learned during the workshop.

2. Parent-Child Communication Activities: Provide parents with activities they can do with their children to improve communication and strengthen their relationships, such as family meetings or communication games.

3. Resource List: Offer a list of resources, including books, websites, and local organizations, that parents can turn to for additional support in conflict management.

Follow-up and Support

1. Q&A Sessions: Allow time for a question-and-answer session where parents can seek advice on specific challenges.

2. Feedback Surveys: Distribute feedback surveys at the end of the workshop to gather insights on what was most beneficial and what could be improved.

3. Continued Learning Opportunities: Inform parents of upcoming workshops, support groups, or other resources for continued learning and conflict management support.

Parent workshops on conflict management skills are a powerful way to engage parents in the educational community. They provide them with the tools they need to effectively support their children's social and emotional development. By focusing on relevant content, interactive learning, and practical applications, schools can empower parents to navigate conflicts constructively, contributing to a positive and supportive family and school environment.

The Role of Parents in Mediating Student Conflicts at Home

The role of parents in mediating student conflicts at home is crucial for developing healthy conflict-resolution skills and fostering a supportive family environment. Disputes among siblings or between children and parents are natural, but how they are addressed can significantly impact children's emotional development and understanding of healthy relationships. Parents can mediate conflicts effectively by adopting strategies that encourage communication, learning, and problem-solving.

Modeling Constructive Conflict Resolution

Parents are the prominent people who provide examples of behavior, especially how to handle Conflict. Demonstrating constructive conflict resolution—such as calm discussion, active listening, and seeking mutually acceptable solutions—teaches children valuable lessons about handling disputes respectfully and effectively.

Facilitating Open Communication

Encouraging open communication is essential in mediating conflicts. Children can share their feelings, thoughts, and concerns in a secure area created by parents where they won't feel judged or punished. This involves teaching children to articulate their emotions and listen to others' perspectives, fostering empathy and understanding among family members.

Encouraging Problem-Solving

During disagreements, parents can help kids learn how to solve problems by determining the main issue, brainstorming several alternatives, and deciding on a plan of action. This approach empowers children to take ownership of their conflicts and work collaboratively towards resolution, building their confidence and independence.

Teaching Emotional Regulation

Conflicts often arise or escalate due to unmanaged emotions. Children can learn techniques for controlling their feelings from their parents, like deep breathing, counting to 10, or stepping away from the situation. Children can approach conflicts more rationally and constructively by learning to manage their emotions.

Setting Clear Boundaries and Expectations

Establishing clear boundaries and expectations regarding behavior during conflicts is essential. Parents should communicate what is acceptable and what is not, such as using respectful language and prohibiting physical aggression. Consistently enforcing these boundaries teaches children the importance of respect and self-control.

Promoting Empathy and Perspective-Taking

Encouraging children to consider the other person's perspective can help de-escalate conflicts and lead to more empathetic resolutions. Parents can facilitate this by asking children to express what they think the other person might be feeling or why they might have acted in a certain way. This helps develop empathy, a critical skill for healthy interpersonal relationships.

Utilizing Neutral Third Parties

In some cases, bringing in a neutral third party, such as another family member or a professional mediator, can help resolve more complex or persistent conflicts. This person can help discover a just resolution by providing a new viewpoint and facilitating a more objective conversation.

Reflecting on Conflicts

After resolving a conflict, parents can encourage reflection on what happened, what was learned, and how similar situations might be handled better. This reflection process helps children internalize the conflict resolution skills they've practiced and understand the positive outcomes of constructive conflict management.

Fostering a Culture of Forgiveness and Reconciliation

Finally, promoting a culture of forgiveness and reconciliation within the family is essential. Encouraging children to apologize and make amends fosters healing and strengthens relationships after conflicts. This teaches children the value of forgiveness, not as a sign of weakness but as an act of compassion and understanding.

Parents play a pivotal role in mediating student conflicts at home, teaching valuable life skills beyond family dynamics into school and future relationships. By modeling positive conflict resolution, fostering open communication, supporting problem-solving, and promoting empathy and forgiveness, parents may assist their children in navigating conflicts and laying the groundwork for healthy emotional development and interpersonal connections.

Collaborative Problem-Solving

Collaborative problem-solving that engages parents in school decisions creates a partnership that benefits students, schools, and families. This approach recognizes parents as critical stakeholders in their children's education and leverages their insights, experiences, and resources to address challenges and capitalize on opportunities. Together, parents and schools can create inclusive, creative, and more successful solutions that meet the needs and goals of the whole school community.

198

Establishing Communication Platforms

To facilitate collaborative problem-solving, schools need to establish effective communication platforms that enable easy and open dialogue with parents. This might include digital tools like school apps, email newsletters, social media groups, online forums, and traditional methods like phone calls and in-person meetings. Ensuring two-way, regular, and inclusive communication is crucial for keeping parents informed and engaged.

Creating Parent Advisory Councils

Parent advisory councils are a formal way to involve parents in school decision-making processes. These councils can bridge the broader parent community and school leadership, providing a structured forum for discussing issues, proposing solutions, and advising on school policies and initiatives. Membership should be diverse to reflect the school's demographic makeup, ensuring that different perspectives are represented.

Involving Parents in Committees and Working Groups

Schools can involve parents in committees and working groups focused on specific areas such as curriculum development, health and safety, extracurricular activities, and community outreach. Involving parents brings fresh ideas and can increase the sense of ownership and commitment to school initiatives.

Organizing Collaborative Workshops and Seminars

Parent involvement can benefit from workshops and seminars that address common educational challenges and opportunities. These events can focus on topics like enhancing learning at home, understanding educational standards, or integrating technology into education. Collaborative workshops encourage the exchange of knowledge and strategies between educators and parents, fostering a unified approach to supporting student success.

Facilitating Focus Groups and Feedback Sessions

Conducting focus groups and feedback sessions with parents provides valuable insights into their perceptions, experiences, and suggestions regarding school operations and policies. This feedback can inform decision-making, highlight improvement areas, and identify innovation opportunities. Ensuring that feedback mechanisms are accessible and responsive encourages ongoing parent participation.

Jointly Developing School Improvement Plans

Engaging parents in developing school improvement plans ensures that these plans address the needs and priorities of the entire school community. Collaboration can take place through surveys, planning workshops, and review meetings. Parents' contributions can enrich planning, making strategies more comprehensive and aligned with community values.

Training for Effective Collaboration

Offering training sessions for parents and school staff on effective collaboration, communication, and conflict resolution can enhance the quality of partnerships. Training can cover topics such as collaborative decision-making processes, how to give and receive constructive feedback, and strategies for building consensus.

Recognizing and Celebrating Contributions

Acknowledging and celebrating parents' contributions to school decisions and initiatives is essential for sustaining engagement. Recognition can be formal, such as awards or public acknowledgments, or informal, such as thank-you notes or mentions in school communications. Celebrating successes together strengthens the school community and reinforces the value of collaborative efforts.

Collaborative problem-solving with parent engagement in school decisions fosters a sense of community, leverages diverse perspectives, and enriches the educational experience for students. By establishing effective communication, creating formal structures for parent involvement, organizing collaborative events, and recognizing contributions, schools can build strong partnerships with parents that drive positive change and support student achievement.

Navigating Special Education Needs

Navigating special education needs collaboratively involves parents, educators, and specialists working together to support students with disabilities or learning differences. This partnership is crucial for developing, implementing, and adjusting Individualized Education Programs (IEPs) or 504 plans that cater to each student's unique needs. A collaborative approach ensures that special education services comply with legal requirements and are genuinely supportive of students' educational and personal growth.

Building Effective Communication Channels

There must be constant, open contact between all sides. Regularly scheduled meetings, progress reports, and accessible contact methods ensure that information flows freely and that concerns or changes can be addressed promptly. Digital platforms can supplement face-to-face interactions, offering a convenient way to share updates, resources, and feedback.

Involving Parents and Guardians

Parents and guardians bring invaluable insights into their child's needs, strengths, and challenges. Their involvement in setting goals, choosing interventions, and evaluating progress ensures that the educational approach aligns with the student's best interests. Schools can facilitate this involvement by providing clear information about unique education processes, rights, and resources available to families.

Utilizing a Team-Based Approach

A multidisciplinary team, including special education teachers, general education teachers, school psychologists, therapists, and other specialists, ensures a holistic understanding of the student's needs. This team collaborates to develop and implement comprehensive educational plans, integrating academic, social, emotional, and physical supports as needed.

Creating Individualized Education Programs (IEPs)

The IEP process is central to special education. It outlines tailored educational objectives and the specific services and supports the student will receive. Collaborative IEP meetings allow team members, including the student, when appropriate, to contribute their perspectives and expertise. This collaborative planning ensures the IEP is ambitious and achievable, promoting the student's continuous growth.

Adapting and Flexibility

It is vital to recognize that students' needs may change over time. The collaborative approach is inherently flexible, allowing adjustments to educational plans based on ongoing assessments and feedback. This adaptability ensures that support remains relevant and practical, helping students overcome challenges and reach their potential.

Professional Development and Training

Educators and school staff benefit from professional development opportunities that enhance their understanding of special education needs and effective strategies for meeting them. Training in collaborative practices, inclusive teaching methods, and the latest educational technologies can improve the support quality for students with special education needs.

Engaging with External Resources and Communities

Collaboration can extend beyond the school, involving external resources such as educational consultants, advocacy groups, and community organizations that support students with disabilities. These partnerships can bring additional expertise, resources, and support to the academic team, enriching the school's unique education program.

Fostering Inclusivity and Respect

A collaborative approach to special education emphasizes inclusivity and respect for diversity. A sense of community and belonging is fostered by initiatives to incorporate special education students into general education classes, extracurricular activities, and school-wide events. Respect for each student's abilities and potential drives the collaborative effort, ensuring all students are valued and supported.

Navigating special education needs through a collaborative approach empowers students, respects families, and enriches the educational community. By prioritizing effective communication, involving parents and guardians, utilizing a team-based approach, adapting to changing needs, and engaging with external resources, schools can provide robust support that meets the diverse needs of students with special education needs, facilitating their academic success and personal development.

Success Stories

Success Story 1: The Mediation Workshop

In a diverse urban school, recurring conflicts between parents and the school administration regarding language services for non-English speaking families had created tension. To address this, the school organized a mediation workshop facilitated by a local university's conflict resolution center. The workshop included parents, teachers, administrators, and students as participants.

The workshop illuminated the communication barriers and misunderstandings contributing to the conflicts through guided discussions, role-playing, and problem-solving exercises. As a result, a bilingual parent liaison position was created to improve communication between the school and non-English-speaking families. The school also launched a series of language classes for parents and staff, fostering a more inclusive and understanding school community.

Success Story 2: The IEP Collaboration Initiative

A small-town school faced challenges with the IEP process, often resulting in disagreements between parents of students with special needs and school staff. The school responded by initiating an IEP Collaboration Program, which paired parents with a special education advocate from the start of the IEP process.

The advocates, trained in special education law and collaborative negotiation, helped bridge the gap between parents and educators, ensuring that all voices were heard and considered. This initiative resolved existing conflicts and preempted potential disputes, leading to more effective and supportive IEPs for students.

Success Story 3: Digital Communication Platform

A suburban high school introduced a digital communication platform to address frequent conflicts arising from miscommunication about student progress and behavior. The platform allowed real-time updates, direct messaging between parents and teachers, and a space for sharing educational resources.

Parents received training on the platform, and teachers committed to regular updates. The transparency and ease of communication reduced misunderstandings significantly, leading to quicker resolutions when issues did arise. The platform became crucial for parent-school collaboration, improving the overall school climate.

Success Story 4: The Parent-Teacher Partnership Program

Recognizing that conflicts often stemmed from a lack of understanding and trust, an inner-city elementary school launched the Parent-Teacher Partnership Program. This initiative paired each parent with a teacher partner for the school year, facilitating regular, informal check-ins in addition to traditional parent-teacher conferences.

This program allowed parents and teachers to build personal relationships, share insights about students' needs and behaviors, and collaboratively address issues before they escalated into conflicts. The initiative was praised for transforming the school's culture, making it more welcoming and cohesive.

Success Story 5: The Conflict Resolution Ambassadors

A rural middle school trained students as Conflict Resolution Ambassadors, focusing on peer mediation techniques. When conflicts arose between parents and the school, these ambassadors facilitated initial discussions, helping to clarify misunderstandings and identify common ground.

This innovative approach empowered students and provided a neutral ground for parents and school staff to begin resolving their conflicts. The presence of student mediators reminded everyone of the shared goal: creating the best possible learning environment. This program led to a significant decrease in parent-school conflicts and became a model for other schools in the district.

These success stories emphasize the value of creative, cooperative approaches to problem-solving between schools and parents. By prioritizing communication, understanding, and mutual respect, schools can turn potential conflicts into opportunities to strengthen partnerships and enhance the educational experience for all students.

Developing Parental Involvement Policies for Conflict Resolution

Developing parental involvement policies for conflict resolution is a strategic approach that schools can adopt to ensure that conflicts are managed effectively, with the engagement and support of parents. These rules recognize parents' crucial role in their children's education and well-being and set explicit norms and processes for their involvement in the resolution process. By formalizing the participation of parents, schools can foster a collaborative environment where conflicts are resolved constructively and with the best interests of students in mind.

Principles of the Policy

1. Transparency: The policy should emphasize the importance of clear, open communication between the school and parents regarding conflict resolution processes.

2. Respect and Fairness: All parties involved in a conflict should be treated fairly, and their voices should be heard and considered.

3. Collaboration: The policy should encourage collaborative approaches to conflict resolution and highlight the value of parental insights and contributions.

4. Confidentiality: Maintaining the confidentiality of students and families involved in conflicts is crucial to protecting their privacy and dignity.

Key Components of the Policy

1. Definition of Conflicts: Clearly define what constitutes a conflict within the school context, including the types of disputes the policy covers.

2. Roles and Responsibilities: Outline the roles and responsibilities of parents, students, teachers, and administrators in the conflict resolution process. This includes how parents will be informed and involved in resolving disputes.

3. Communication Procedures: Specify the procedures for communicating conflicts to parents, including timelines and the methods of communication to be used.

4. Resolution Process: Detail the steps of the conflict resolution process, including initial assessment, mediation, or intervention strategies, and how decisions will be made. The process should allow for parental input and participation at each stage.

5. Training and Resources: Commit to providing parents with training on conflict resolution skills and strategies and resources to support them in navigating conflicts effectively.

6. Monitoring and Evaluation: Include provisions for monitoring the implementation of the policy and evaluating its effectiveness in resolving conflicts and involving parents. This could involve regular surveys of parents and staff and reviews of conflict resolution outcomes.

7. Feedback Mechanism: Establish a mechanism for parents and school staff to provide feedback on the conflict resolution process, ensuring that the policy remains responsive to the school community's needs.

8. Revisions and Updates: The policy ought to be periodically reviewed and revised to consider new laws and regulations and modifications in the needs of the school community.

Implementation Strategies

1. Policy Dissemination: Ensure the parental involvement policy for conflict resolution is widely disseminated and easily accessible to all parents and school staff. This can be achieved through the school website, parent-teacher meetings, and school newsletters.

2. Parent Education: Organize workshops, seminars, or information sessions for parents to educate them about the policy, conflict resolution techniques, and how they can effectively contribute to resolving disputes.

3. Collaboration with Parent Organizations: Engage with parent-teacher associations and other parent organizations in the development and implementation of the policy to ensure it aligns with the needs and expectations of parents.

4. Professional Development for Staff: Provide ongoing professional development for school staff on engaging parents in conflict resolution, emphasizing communication skills, cultural competency, and collaborative problem-solving.

Developing a parental involvement policy for conflict resolution is a proactive step schools can take to enhance the partnership between parents and the school. By establishing clear guidelines and procedures for involving parents in conflict resolution, schools can leverage families' unique perspectives and strengths to create a more positive, supportive, and effective learning environment for students.

CHAPTER 12

LEGAL AND ETHICAL CONSIDERATIONS IN CONFLICT RESOLUTION

U nderstanding the legal frameworks impacting school conflicts is crucial for administrators, educators, and parents. These frameworks set the boundaries within which conflicts must be managed and resolved, ensuring that the rights of all parties are respected and that the school environment remains conducive to learning. Legal considerations can significantly influence how discipline, special education, discrimination, and privacy conflicts are addressed. By familiarizing themselves with these legal frameworks, school stakeholders can navigate disputes more effectively, avoiding potential legal pitfalls and fostering a culture of fairness and respect.

Discipline and Student Rights

School discipline is governed by complex laws and regulations designed to protect students' rights while maintaining order and safety. For instance, the Individuals with Disabilities Education Act (IDEA) in the United States provides specific protections for students with disabilities, including the requirement for a manifestation determination review before any disciplinary action that could result in a change of placement for more than ten days. Understanding these legal requirements ensures that disciplinary actions are effective, equitable, and in compliance with federal and state laws.

Special Education Laws

The IDEA and Section 504 of the Rehabilitation Act are critical legal frameworks governing the provision of special education services and accommodations. These laws require schools to offer a free appropriate public education (FAPE) to students with disabilities in the least restrictive environment (LRE). Conflicts often arise around developing and implementing Individualized Education Programs (IEPs) or 504 plans. Familiarity with these legal frameworks helps schools navigate such disputes, ensuring that students receive the support they need while upholding their legal rights.

Anti-discrimination Laws

Title VI of the Civil Rights Act, Title IX of the Education Amendments, and the Americans with Disabilities Act (ADA) are just a few examples of federal and state anti-discrimination laws that forbid discrimination in educational programs and activities based on race, color, national origin, sex, disability, and other protected characteristics. These laws impact how schools address conflicts related to bullying, harassment, and equal access to educational opportunities. Schools must have policies and procedures to promptly and effectively address allegations of discrimination, ensuring compliance with these laws and fostering an inclusive school environment.

Privacy Laws

Privacy legislation, like the Family Educational Rights and Privacy Act (FERPA) in the United States, protects the confidentiality of student education records. Conflicts involving the sharing of sensitive information or access to student records must be handled with an understanding of FERPA's provisions. These provisions grant parents certain rights to access and amend their children's education records and set strict limits on disclosing those records without parental consent. Schools must balance the need for transparency and communication with parents with the legal requirement to protect student privacy.

Developing Policies and Training

Schools should develop clear policies and procedures that reflect current laws and best practices to manage legal risks associated with school conflicts effectively. This includes policies on discipline, bullying and harassment, special education, and privacy. School personnel must receive regular training on these rules and the underlying legal concepts to guarantee that conflicts are addressed in a way that is efficient and compliant with the law.

Seeking Legal Counsel

Given the complexity of the legal landscape, schools should not hesitate to seek advice from legal counsel when navigating brutal conflicts. Legal professionals can guide compliance issues, represent the school in disputes, and offer training on legal matters affecting schools. This partnership can be invaluable in managing conflicts effectively and avoiding potential legal challenges.

Understanding the legal frameworks impacting school conflicts empowers school stakeholders to resolve disputes in a manner that is respectful, fair, and in line with both educational best practices and legal requirements. This knowledge is essential for creating a school environment where every student can thrive, free from discrimination, undue disciplinary measures, and privacy violations.

Navigating Ethical Dilemmas in School Conflict Resolution

Navigating ethical dilemmas in school conflict resolution requires a thoughtful and conscientious approach. Ethical dilemmas often arise when competing interests, values, or principles are at stake, and resolving them necessitates careful consideration of all involved parties' rights, needs, and well-being. School administrators, teachers, and conflict resolution professionals must balance legal obligations, educational policies, and the broader ethical implications of their decisions. Here are strategies for effectively addressing ethical dilemmas in school conflict resolution.

Establishing Ethical Guidelines

The first step in navigating ethical dilemmas is establishing moral guidelines or principles to inform decision-making processes. These include fairness, respect for all parties, confidentiality, and a commitment to the best interests of the students. Having clear guidelines helps ensure that decisions are consistent and grounded in the school's core values.

Engaging in Reflective Practice

Reflective practice involves taking the time to consider the ethical dimensions of a conflict and the potential impact of different resolution strategies. This might include asking questions such as: "Who will be affected by this decision?" "What are the possible long- and short-term effects?" and "Is this choice consistent with our code of ethics?" Reflecting on these questions can help illuminate the most ethically sound path forward.

Seeking Multiple Perspectives

Ethical dilemmas are often complex, with no clear right or wrong answers. Seeking input from multiple perspectives can provide a more comprehensive understanding of the issue. This might involve consulting with colleagues, engaging with parents and students, or seeking advice from legal or ethical experts. Understanding different viewpoints can aid in making more informed and balanced decisions.

Prioritizing Transparency and Communication

Transparency and open communication are crucial when navigating ethical dilemmas. This means being honest about the dilemma's nature, the decision-making process, and the rationale behind the final decision. Clear communication can help manage expectations, reduce misunderstandings, and build trust among all parties.

Focusing on Restorative Practices

In contrast to punitive methods, therapeutic techniques prioritize relationship restoration and harm repair. When facing ethical dilemmas, considering restorative approaches can often provide solutions that address the needs of all parties and contribute to a more positive and supportive school environment. This might involve facilitated dialogue, mediation, or other processes that allow those affected by the conflict to express their feelings, discuss the impact, and collaboratively determine how to move forward.

Documenting Decision-Making Processes

Documenting the decision-making process, including the ethical considerations involved, the perspectives sought, and the rationale for the final decision, is essential for accountability and learning. This paperwork can show the school's dedication to making moral decisions and be a reference for future disputes.

Providing Training and Support

Providing staff with training and support on ethical decision-making and conflict resolution can strengthen the school's capacity to navigate ethical dilemmas. This might include professional development workshops, access to resources on ethics in education, and opportunities for staff to discuss and reflect on ethical challenges they have faced.

Reviewing and Adjusting Policies

Finally, reviewing and adjusting school policies to ensure they reflect ethical principles and best practices in conflict resolution is essential. This ongoing process helps ensure that the school's approach to conflict resolution remains responsive to the community's needs and aligned with ethical standards.

Navigating ethical dilemmas in school conflict resolution is a challenging but essential part of creating a respectful, just, and supportive educational environment. By establishing ethical guidelines, engaging in reflective practice, seeking multiple perspectives, prioritizing transparency, focusing on restorative practices, documenting decisions, providing training, and reviewing policies, schools can navigate these dilemmas with integrity and care.

Confidentiality and Privacy Considerations in Mediation

Confidentiality and privacy considerations are cornerstone elements in the mediation process, ensuring that the parties involved feel safe discussing their concerns openly and working towards a resolution. These principles not only protect the participants' interests but also enhance mediation's effectiveness by fostering an environment of trust and Openness. Here's a closer look at how confidentiality and privacy are maintained in mediation and why they are so important.

The Importance of Confidentiality in Mediation

1. Encourages Openness: Knowing that the details of their discussions will remain confidential encourages participants to speak freely, share sensitive information, and explore resolution options without fear of external judgment or repercussions.

2. Protects Participants: Confidentiality protects the reputations and relationships of the parties involved, preventing the potential harm from public disclosure of sensitive issues.

3. Preserves Integrity of the Process: The assurance of confidentiality helps maintain the integrity of the mediation process, making it a trustworthy and credible method for dispute resolution.

4. Legal and Ethical Obligations: Many places have laws or ethical codes requiring mediators to keep mediation sessions private unless there are exceptional circumstances like threats of danger or obligations to reveal material under the law.

Strategies for Ensuring Confidentiality

1. Confidentiality Agreements: Participants, including the mediator, often sign confidentiality agreements at the outset of the mediation process. These agreements clearly outline what information is considered confidential and any exceptions to confidentiality.

2. Private Sessions: Mediation sessions are conducted privately, and access to mediation records is strictly controlled. This ensures that discussions are not overheard and documents are inaccessible to unauthorized individuals.

3. Secure Communication Channels: Secure channels are utilized when electronic communication is part of mediation to preserve participant privacy and the secrecy of any information shared.

4. Clear Guidelines on Information Sharing: Mediators establish clear guidelines on how information shared during mediation can be used. For example, information disclosed in mediation may not be admissible in court proceedings unless all parties agree.

5. Training and Professional Standards: Mediators undergo training that strongly focuses on confidentiality and privacy issues. Professional standards and ethical codes also guide mediators in maintaining confidentiality.

Exceptions to Confidentiality

While confidentiality is a fundamental aspect of mediation, there are exceptions where disclosure may be required by law or necessary to prevent harm. These exceptions might include:

- **Threats of violence or harm:** If a participant threatens violence or harm to themselves or others, the mediator may have a duty to report this information to the appropriate authorities.
- **Child abuse or neglect:** Allegations or evidence of child abuse or neglect disclosed during mediation typically must be reported to child protection agencies.
- **Legal obligations:** In some cases, the law may require mediators to disclose certain information, such as during legal proceedings or investigations.

Understanding and respecting confidentiality and privacy considerations are critical for all parties involved in mediation. By ensuring these principles are upheld, mediation can provide a secure, trusted platform for resolving disputes in a respectful, effective manner that protects the participants' interests.

Legal Obligations in Addressing Bullying and Cyberbullying

Schools have a significant responsibility to address bullying and cyberbullying, guided by both federal laws and state statutes that underline the importance of providing a safe learning environment. Bullying is not explicitly prohibited by federal law. Still, several legislation, such as the Civil Rights Act of 1964, the Education Amendments of 1972, and the Americans with Disabilities Act of 1990, require schools to deal with discriminatory harassment. This encompasses behaviors that can be identified as bullying, particularly when they interfere with a student's access to education based on race, color, national origin, sex, or disability.

State laws across the United States further specify the actions schools must take against bullying and cyberbullying. These laws often require the development of anti-bullying policies, procedures for reporting and responding to incidents, and staff training on prevention. These laws vary significantly but collectively emphasize the need for schools to actively work towards eradicating bullying behaviors.

In fulfilling these legal obligations, schools must implement comprehensive prevention programs that educate the entire school community about the detrimental effects of bullying and encourage positive social behaviors. They are also tasked with responding promptly to bullying incidents. This includes conducting thorough investigations, taking appropriate disciplinary action against perpetrators, and ensuring such behavior is not repeated. Moreover, providing support for victims is paramount, which may involve offering counseling services, adjusting their educational environment, and putting protective measures in place to prevent future harassment.

Teachers and other school employees are essential to this process. They should receive ongoing training to recognize the signs of bullying and understand the best practices for intervention and support. Engaging parents and the broader community is also critical. Schools should offer guidance on recognizing bullying behaviors and provide resources to support children in dealing with and preventing bullying and cyberbullying.

Through these concerted efforts, schools adhere to legal requirements and foster a culture of respect, safety, and support, ensuring that all students can learn and grow in a nurturing environment.

The Role of School Policies in Conflict Resolution Ethics

The role of school policies in conflict resolution ethics is pivotal in establishing a framework that guides how conflicts are managed and resolved within the educational setting. These policies serve as a blueprint for ethical conduct, ensuring that all parties involved in a dispute are treated fairly, respectfully, and with dignity. School policies play a crucial role in creating a positive and respectful learning environment by clearly outlining the principles, procedures, and expectations for conflict resolution.

At the heart of these policies is the commitment to ethical principles such as transparency, impartiality, and confidentiality. Transparency ensures that the conflict resolution process is open and understandable to all involved, fostering trust in the system. Impartiality guarantees that all parties receive a fair hearing, free from bias or favoritism. At the same time, confidentiality protects the privacy and dignity of those involved, encouraging Openness and honesty in the resolution process.

School policies typically include procedures for reporting conflicts, steps for investigation, and mechanisms for resolution, ranging from mediation to disciplinary action. These procedures are designed to address conflicts efficiently and uphold the ethical standards of the school community. School policies help prevent misunderstandings and ensure that conflicts are handled consistently and fairly by providing clear guidelines.

Furthermore, rather than emphasizing punitive measures, these policies frequently promote therapeutic methods, which concentrate on mending harm and restoring relationships. This approach aligns with ethical principles by fostering understanding, accountability, and reconciliation, contributing to a more supportive and cohesive school community.

In addition to governing the resolution of conflicts, school policies also play a vital role in conflict prevention. They can involve offering staff and students instruction and training in conflict resolution techniques and encouraging an environment of open dialogue, respect, and problem-solving. This proactive stance on conflict resolution ethics helps minimize conflicts and enriches the educational experience for students, preparing them with valuable life skills.

Furthermore, school policies provide a framework for involving parents and the broader community in conflict resolution processes. Engaging these stakeholders ensures that a wide range of perspectives is considered and that the school's approach to conflict resolution is aligned with the values and expectations of the broader community. This collaborative approach reinforces the ethical foundation of school policies, ensuring they are responsive, inclusive, and effective.

School policies' role in conflict resolution ethics is multifaceted and essential. By establishing clear, moral guidelines for managing and resolving conflicts, these policies ensure that all school community members are treated with fairness, respect, and dignity. Through a commitment to transparency, impartiality, confidentiality, restorative practices, and community engagement, school policies foster a positive, respectful, and supportive learning environment where students can thrive.

Case Study Analysis: Legal Challenges in School Conflicts

In a suburban school district, a significant legal challenge arose involving a conflict between the administration and a group of parents over handling bullying incidents. The parents claimed the school had not taken adequate steps to protect their children from repeated bullying, alleging negligence and a failure to provide a safe learning environment, as required by state anti-bullying laws and the school's policies. This case underscores the complexities and legal ramifications of managing school conflicts and highlights the importance of adherence to legal standards and proactive communication in conflict resolution.

Background

The conflict originated when several students reported being bullied by peers over an extended period. Despite these reports, the parents believed the school's response was insufficient, with minimal action taken against the perpetrators and a lack of support offered to the victims. Feeling their concerns were not adequately addressed, the parents filed a legal complaint against the school district, alleging that the school's inaction violated their children's rights to a safe, educational environment.

Legal Framework

The legal challenge centered on the state's anti-bullying laws, which mandate schools to implement comprehensive anti-bullying policies, including procedures for reporting, investigating, and addressing bullying incidents. The case also entailed issues under federal statutes, including the Education Amendments of 1972's Title IX, because of the nature of several bullying events, which included harassment based on gender.

Analysis

The case presented several critical issues for analysis:

1.   **Compliance with Anti-Bullying Laws**: The school's adherence to state anti-bullying laws and policies was scrutinized. The investigation revealed gaps in implementing the reporting and response procedures outlined in the school's anti-bullying policy.

2.   **Duty of Care**: Central to the case was the school's duty of care to protect students from harm. The legal challenge highlighted the need for schools to take proactive and effective measures to fulfill this duty beyond merely having policies in place.

3.   **Communication and Transparency**: The conflict was exacerbated by perceived poor communication between the school and the concerned parents. The parents felt their reports of bullying were not taken seriously, and there was a lack of transparency regarding the steps the school was taking to address the issue.

4.   **Restorative Practices**: The absence of restorative practices in the school's response was noted. Such practices could have offered a more comprehensive approach to addressing the bullying, focusing on repairing harm and restoring relationships rather than punitive measures alone.

Resolution

The legal challenge prompted the school district to reevaluate its handling of bullying incidents. In settling the case, the school agreed to undertake several actions, including:

- Revising its anti-bullying policies to comply with state laws and best practices fully.

- Implementing additional training for staff on identifying, reporting, and addressing bullying.
- Improving communication with parents regarding incidents of bullying and the measures taken in response.
- Introducing restorative practices as part of its strategy to prevent and address bullying, fostering a more positive school climate.

This case study emphasizes the crucial importance of following the law, communicating clearly, and using therapeutic techniques to resolve school problems. It highlights the potential legal challenges schools may face when conflicts are not managed adequately and the need for schools to proactively address issues of bullying and harassment to fulfill their duty of care to students. By learning from this case, schools can better navigate the complexities of conflict resolution in a legally sound and educationally beneficial manner.

Developing Ethical Guidelines for Conflict Resolution in Schools

Developing ethical guidelines for conflict resolution in schools is a proactive step toward ensuring that disputes are handled with fairness, integrity, and respect for all involved parties. These guidelines serve as a moral compass, guiding educators, administrators, students, and parents through the complexities of conflict resolution in a way that prioritizes the well-being and rights of individuals while fostering a positive school culture. Creating a comprehensive set of ethical guidelines involves several key considerations and steps, blending the school's values with best practices in conflict resolution.

Principles of Ethical Conflict Resolution

The foundation of ethical guidelines is a set of core principles that reflect the school's commitment to ethical conduct. These might include:

- Respect for all individuals: Recognizing the dignity and worth of every person involved in a conflict, ensuring that all voices are heard and considered.
- Fairness and justice: Ensuring that the conflict resolution process is impartial and equitable, offering equal opportunities for all parties to present their perspectives.
- Confidentiality: Protecting the privacy of individuals involved in conflicts, ensuring that sensitive information is handled with discretion.
- Transparency: Being transparent and open about the conflict resolution process, including the steps involved, the criteria used for decision-making, and the rationale behind final decisions.
- Accountability: Holding all parties, including the school, accountable for their actions and decisions in the resolution process.
- Empathy and understanding: Encouraging a genuine attempt to understand the feelings, needs, and viewpoints of others involved in the conflict.

Developing the Guidelines

1. Collaborative Development: Involve a diverse group of stakeholders in developing the ethical guidelines, including educators, administrators, students, parents, and possibly community members. This ensures that the guidelines reflect the values and needs of the entire school community.

2. Review Existing Policies and Laws: Examine current school policies and relevant laws to ensure that the ethical guidelines align with legal requirements and existing standards of conduct.

3. Address Various Types of Conflicts: Consider the range of conflicts that may arise in a school setting, from interpersonal disputes to bullying, discrimination, and grievances against the school. The guidelines should provide ethical direction for resolving these conflicts.

4. Specify Procedures and Practices: While the guidelines will be grounded in principles, they should also offer practical direction on ethical practices and procedures for conflict resolution. This might include steps for reporting conflicts, guidelines for mediation or negotiation, and criteria for involving external parties.

5. Training and Education: Develop training programs for school staff, students, and parents on the ethical guidelines and the importance of ethical conduct in conflict resolution. This education can be integrated into professional development programs, classroom instruction, and parent engagement initiatives.

6. Implementation and Monitoring: Clearly define the roles and responsibilities of school personnel in implementing the ethical guidelines. Establish mechanisms for monitoring adherence to these guidelines and addressing unethical conduct.

7. Review and Update: Regularly review the ethical guidelines to assess their effectiveness and relevance. Solicit feedback from the school community to identify areas for improvement and update the guidelines as needed to reflect changes in the school environment or broader societal norms.

Developing ethical guidelines for conflict resolution is a critical step in promoting a culture of fairness, respect, and empathy in schools. By establishing clear principles and practices for addressing conflicts, schools can ensure that disputes are resolved in a manner that upholds the dignity and rights of all individuals involved. These guidelines not only guide the school community through the resolution process but also contribute to students' moral and social development, preparing them to navigate conflicts ethically and constructively beyond the school setting.

CHAPTER 13

CONFLICT RESOLUTION ACROSS THE CURRICULUM

Integrating conflict resolution into STEM (Science, Technology, Engineering, and Mathematics) education represents a holistic approach to learning that prepares students not only academically but also socially for the challenges of the future. This integration acknowledges that navigating and resolving conflicts is as crucial as technical skills in these fields. By weaving conflict resolution into STEM curricula, educators can foster environments that encourage collaboration, critical thinking, and effective communication among students.

One effective method is through project-based learning, a staple in STEM education, which naturally lends itself to teaching conflict resolution. Students inevitably encounter differing opinions and approaches when working on group projects. Educators can use these moments to guide students through negotiation and compromise, emphasizing the importance of listening, empathy, and finding mutually beneficial solutions.

Incorporating role-playing exercises into the STEM classroom can also be beneficial. These exercises can simulate real-world scenarios where conflicts might arise in a scientific or technological context, such as disagreements over project directions, resource allocation, or ethical considerations in research. Through role-playing, students can practice navigating these conflicts, gain insights into others' perspectives, and develop strategies for resolution.

Peer teaching and collaborative learning are other avenues for integrating conflict resolution into STEM education. These methods encourage students to explain concepts to one another, work together to solve problems, and manage the group dynamics that arise. Such activities naturally foster a setting where conflict resolution skills are needed and developed as students learn to reconcile different learning styles and perspectives.

Debates on STEM-related topics, particularly those with ethical implications, such as the impact of artificial intelligence on employment or the environmental consequences of specific engineering projects, can also be powerful tools. Students must listen to opposing views, state their opinions correctly, and conduct themselves politely during debates—all essential skills for successful conflict resolution.

Furthermore, integrating discussions about historical conflicts and resolutions within the STEM fields into the curriculum can provide valuable lessons. They analyzed how prominent figures in science and technology navigated intellectual, ethical, or personal disputes, which can offer students insights into the complexity of conflicts and the importance of resolving them constructively.

To support this integrated approach, educators themselves may benefit from professional development opportunities focused on conflict resolution strategies and how to incorporate them into STEM teaching effectively. This ensures they have the skills and knowledge to foster a learning environment that values and teaches conflict resolution alongside academic content.

Finally, creating a classroom culture that values questions, welcomes diverse viewpoints, and treats mistakes as learning opportunities can help normalize conflict as a part of learning and discovery in STEM. This culture encourages students to voice their opinions and concerns openly, knowing that conflicts will be addressed constructively and supportively.

Integrating conflict resolution into STEM education enriches the learning experience, preparing students to be skilled professionals in their chosen fields and effective communicators and problem-solvers. This all-encompassing method gives students the skills they need to lead and prosper in a world that is getting more complicated and collaborative by the day.

Humanities and Social Sciences

Incorporating conflict resolution into humanities and social sciences education offers a profound opportunity to equip students with crucial life skills. These disciplines naturally explore human behavior, society, culture, and history, providing rich contexts for understanding the complexities of conflict and strategies for resolution. By leveraging the content and methodologies inherent in these disciplines, educators can foster students' abilities to navigate disagreements, understand diverse perspectives, and collaborate effectively.

Literature classes, for example, present a unique avenue for teaching conflict resolution. Students can investigate the origins, effects, and different approaches characters take to settle conflicts by analyzing characters, narratives, and settings. Discussing literary conflicts encourages empathy, as students must consider the motivations and feelings of characters different from themselves. Educators can further enrich this learning by guiding students to draw parallels between the conflicts in literature and real-world situations, encouraging them to propose alternative resolutions based on conflict resolution principles.

History lessons also provide valuable lessons in conflict and resolution. They trace the origins of significant disputes, examine the factors that escalated them, and analyze how they were resolved. By studying historical conflicts, students can learn about the importance of negotiation and diplomacy and the often devastating consequences of unresolved disputes. Projects that require students to research and present specific historical disputes focusing on the resolution strategies employed can deepen their understanding of how diverse approaches to conflict resolution can lead to varied outcomes.

Educators can integrate conflict resolution in social studies by examining current events and global issues. This makes learning relevant and engaging and allows students to apply conflict resolution theories to contemporary challenges. Discussions can be structured around identifying the root causes of conflicts, considering the perspectives of different stakeholders, and brainstorming possible solutions. Such activities encourage critical thinking and active engagement with the world's complexities.

Psychology and sociology classes offer insights into conflict's individual and societal aspects, respectively. In psychology, students can learn about the psychological underpinnings of conflict, including emotional triggers and cognitive biases that can lead to or exacerbate disputes. Sociology classes can examine conflicts within and between societies, exploring how social structures, cultural norms, and inequality contribute to conflicts. Assignments can encourage students to apply psychological and sociological theories to develop intervention strategies for hypothetical or real-life conflicts.

Furthermore, philosophy courses provide a space to explore conflict and resolution's ethical considerations. Through studying moral philosophy, students can engage with questions about justice, rights, and the ethical obligations of individuals and societies in conflict situations. Debates and discussions based on philosophical texts can challenge students to consider the moral dimensions of conflict resolution strategies.

To support these educational activities, educators can utilize a variety of pedagogical approaches, including:

- Debate and discussion to encourage students to articulate their viewpoints and consider those of others.

- Role-playing to simulate conflicts and resolution processes, allowing students to practice negotiation and mediation skills.

- Case studies drawn from literature, history, current events, or theoretical scenarios to analyze conflicts and propose solutions.

- Collaborative projects that require students to work together to resolve conflicts, mirroring the collaborative nature of real-world conflict resolution.

In integrating conflict resolution into humanities and social sciences, educators enhance students' understanding of these disciplines and equip them with the skills to thoughtfully and effectively address conflicts in their personal lives and communities. This approach fosters a generation of individuals capable of contributing to a more peaceful, understanding, and collaborative world.

Art and Music as Mediums for Conflict Expression and Resolution

Art and music hold unique power as mediums for both the expression of conflict and the facilitation of its resolution. Through these creative outlets, individuals can explore and convey complex emotions, experiences, and perspectives related to conflict, offering insights that might not be as effectively communicated through words alone—engaging with art and music, whether as creators or observers, provides a cathartic experience that can lead to a deeper understanding of conflicts and pave the way for healing and reconciliation.

In art classes, students can be encouraged to create works that reflect personal or historical conflicts, using visual symbolism to express the nuances of these disputes and their impacts. Such projects allow students to process their feelings about conflicts in a tangible form, fostering empathy and understanding when shared with peers. Similarly, art appreciation lessons can include analyses of artworks that have played roles in social movements or depicted significant conflicts, discussing how these pieces have influenced public perception and contributed to dialogue and change.

Music education offers parallel opportunities for exploring conflict. Composing, performing, and analyzing music that addresses themes of discord and harmony can inspire reflection and discussion among students. Lyrics often explicitly address conflicts, while the structures and harmonies of music can metaphorically represent the dynamics of disputes and resolutions. Group music-making activities, such as ensemble performances or collaborative compositions, inherently involve negotiation and compromise, mirroring the process of conflict resolution and highlighting the importance of cooperation and listening to others.

Furthermore, interdisciplinary projects that combine art, music, and other subjects can enrich students' understanding of conflict and its resolution. For instance, a project might involve creating a multimedia presentation on a specific historical conflict, incorporating research, visual art, and music to explore the conflict's causes, key events, and outcomes. Such projects deepen students' understanding of the conflict and encourage them to consider creative approaches to resolution and peace-building.

Art and music can also serve as bridges between diverse groups, fostering connections and understanding that can mitigate conflicts. School events showcasing art and music from different cultures can celebrate diversity and prompt discussions about the everyday human experiences underlying various forms of expression. Workshops led by guest artists or musicians who have used their work to address conflict and advocate for peace can inspire students to consider how they might use their creative talents for social impact.

The therapeutic aspects of art and music should not be overlooked. For individuals directly affected by conflict, engaging in creative activities can offer a form of healing, helping to process trauma and express emotions that might be difficult to articulate verbally. Schools can collaborate with local arts organizations or therapists to provide workshops or sessions focused on art and music therapy, supporting students' emotional well-being and resilience.

Incorporating art and music as mediums for exploring and resolving conflicts enriches the educational experience, providing students with tools for emotional expression, critical thinking, and empathy. By recognizing the value of these creative outlets in understanding and addressing conflicts, educators can foster a more compassionate, reflective, and innovative student body equipped to contribute to a more harmonious world.

Physical Education and Sports

Physical education and sports play vital roles in teaching students about teamwork and providing practical experiences in resolving conflicts. In these environments, students get physical exercise and acquire essential life skills like teamwork, communication, and fair play. These environments naturally give rise to situations where disagreements and conflicts emerge, whether over the game, the game rule strategies, or competitive tensions. However, the right approach can transform these challenges into powerful learning opportunities.

Teamwork is fundamental in physical education and sports. Students learn to work together towards a common goal, understanding that individual success is often intertwined with the team's performance. This setting fosters a sense of community and belonging, where the emphasis is placed on collective effort rather than individual achievement alone. Through sports, students experience firsthand the importance of supporting one another, sharing responsibilities, and celebrating shared successes, reinforcing teamwork's value in achieving objectives.

Conflict resolution in sports and physical education is equally crucial. Coaches and educators are essential when it comes to helping students work through conflicts that may develop during team selection, gameplay, or competitive circumstances. By encouraging open dialogue, educators can help students express their viewpoints constructively and listen to others' perspectives. This process helps students understand that conflicts can be resolved through communication and compromise without resorting to aggression or resentment.

Educators can enhance these learning experiences by incorporating specific activities to build teamwork and resolve conflicts. For example, cooperative games that require students to work together to solve problems or achieve objectives can highlight the importance of teamwork in a tangible way. Similarly, role-playing scenarios that simulate potential conflicts in sports settings can provide students with a safe space to practice negotiation and mediation skills.

Reflective discussions after games or physical activities offer another valuable teaching tool. These discussions can focus on what went well, what challenges the team faced, and how conflicts were (or were not) successfully resolved. Through guided reflection, students can gain insights into their behavior and decision-making processes, learning from positive outcomes and mistakes.

Significantly, the lessons learned in physical education and sports extend beyond the playing field. The teamwork and conflict resolution skills students develop in these settings are applicable in many other areas of their lives, from academic group projects to future workplace environments. Students are better prepared to navigate the complexities of interpersonal relationships in diverse settings by learning to work collaboratively, communicate effectively, and resolve disagreements constructively.

Moreover, the emphasis on sportsmanship and ethical conduct in physical education and sports teaches students to respect opponents, adhere to rules, and value fairness, further underscoring the importance of ethical behavior in all aspects of life. This holistic approach to education, which integrates physical, social, and moral learning, is essential for developing well-rounded individuals who are physically active and socially and emotionally intelligent.

Physical education and sports offer a dynamic and engaging platform for teaching teamwork and conflict resolution. Through practical experiences in these settings, students learn the value of working together, the skills necessary for resolving conflicts, and the principles of fair play and respect. These invaluable lessons equip students with the tools to succeed on and off the field.

Project-Based Learning and Its Role in Teaching Conflict Resolution

Students are actively involved in the learning process through project-based learning, which consists of exploring problems and difficulties in the real world. Within this framework, students often work in groups to research, design, and implement projects that provide practical solutions. This collaborative nature of project-based learning naturally introduces opportunities for teaching conflict resolution, as students must navigate differing opinions, divide responsibilities, and collectively overcome obstacles to achieve their goals.

The role of project-based learning in teaching conflict resolution is multifaceted. At its core, it encourages students to engage with each other meaningfully, fostering an environment where conflict is recognized as a natural and manageable aspect of collaboration. Students encounter situations during a project that require them to articulate their ideas, listen to others, negotiate roles, and make joint decisions. These situations are practical lessons in resolving conflicts, emphasizing the importance of communication, empathy, and compromise.

One key aspect of project-based learning is its ability to mirror the complexities of real-world interactions. Students learn that differing viewpoints are not only inevitable but can also be valuable. By working through disagreements to find common ground or innovative solutions, students realize that diverse perspectives can contribute to more robust and creative outcomes. This understanding is crucial in conflict resolution, as it moves students from a win-lose mindset to one seeking mutual benefit.

Educators are critical in guiding students through the conflict resolution process within project-based learning. They can model effective communication strategies, facilitate discussions that allow for equitable participation, and provide tools and language for constructive disagreement. Additionally, educators can debrief conflicts with students, helping them reflect on what strategies were effective, what could have been handled differently, and how conflicts led to learning or project advancement.

Incorporating specific conflict resolution training into project-based learning enhances its effectiveness. This can include workshops on active listening, nonviolent communication, or mediation techniques, providing students with a more formal set of skills to apply when conflicts arise. Such training ensures that students are equipped to handle disagreements within the scope of their projects and other areas of their lives.

Furthermore, collaborative projects often result in a tangible product or solution, which can be a powerful reminder of what can be achieved through effective teamwork and conflict resolution. The sense of accomplishment from overcoming challenges and completing a project can reinforce the value of working through conflicts constructively.

Project-based learning also allows for diversity in team composition, which can introduce conflicts stemming from different cultural backgrounds, learning styles, and personal experiences. Navigating these differences teaches students the importance of inclusivity and adaptability, which are essential for conflict resolution in increasingly diverse societal and professional contexts.

The assessment process in project-based learning can further emphasize the importance of conflict resolution. Educators can provide feedback on how effectively students resolve conflicts by evaluating the final product, team dynamics, and problem-solving processes. This approach reinforces that conflict resolution is a valuable skill, integral to personal development and academic achievement.

Project-based learning provides a dynamic and engaging context for teaching conflict resolution. By confronting students with real-world challenges that require collaboration, communication, and compromise, this educational approach equips them with essential life skills. Through the active guidance of educators and targeted conflict resolution training, students learn to navigate disagreements constructively, leading to personal growth and successful project outcomes.

Evaluating Conflict Resolution Education

Evaluating conflict resolution education involves assessing both the effectiveness of the curriculum and the impact of these lessons on

237

students' abilities to manage and resolve conflicts. Given conflict resolution skills' dynamic and interpersonal nature, evaluation requires a multifaceted approach that combines quantitative and qualitative tools and techniques. These assessments not only gauge the immediate outcomes of conflict resolution education but also help understand the long-term benefits and areas for improvement.

Surveys and Questionnaires

Surveys and questionnaires are valuable tools for evaluating students' self-reported skills and attitudes toward conflict resolution. These instruments can measure changes in students' knowledge of conflict resolution strategies, their confidence in using them, and their perceptions of conflict. Surveys can be administered before and after the conflict resolution education program to identify shifts in understanding and attitudes. Including questions that assess specific skills, such as active listening, empathy, and negotiation, can provide insights into the curriculum's impact on these critical areas.

Observations

Direct observation of students in structured settings, like role-playing exercises, and natural settings, such as the classroom or playground, offers concrete evidence of how conflict resolution education translates into behavior. Observers can look for specific indicators of conflict resolution skills, such as using "I" statements, active listening cues, and cooperative problem-solving strategies. These observations can be standardized using checklists or rating scales to ensure consistency and objectivity.

Reflections and Journals

Encouraging students to reflect on their experiences with conflict and conflict resolution in journals can provide deep insights into how they internalize and apply what they've learned. Reflections can reveal students' thought processes during conflicts, their emotional responses, and their evaluations of the outcomes of their conflict resolution efforts. Analyzing these reflections can help educators understand the nuances of students' learning experiences and identify areas where additional support might be needed.

Peer and Teacher Feedback

Collecting feedback from peers and teachers about students' behavior and conflict-resolution skills can offer additional perspectives on the effectiveness of the education program. This feedback can be gathered informally through discussions or more formally through surveys and feedback forms. Peer and teacher feedback can highlight how students apply conflict resolution skills in real-life situations and how these skills affect their relationships and classroom dynamics.

Conflict Resolution Scenarios

Administering pre- and post-tests that involve analyzing conflict resolution scenarios can assess students' ability to apply theoretical knowledge in practical situations. These scenarios can ask students to identify the conflict, propose potential solutions, and predict the outcomes of different approaches. Comparing responses before and after the conflict resolution education program can indicate growth in students' analytical and problem-solving skills.

Interviews

Interviewing students, teachers, and parents can yield qualitative data about the perceived effectiveness of conflict resolution education. Interviews can explore participants' overall satisfaction with the program, perceived changes in students' behaviors, and suggestions for improvement. This approach allows for an extensive comprehension of the effects of conflict resolution education on the school community.

Longitudinal Studies

Long-term follow-up with students who have participated in conflict resolution education can provide insights into the lasting impact of these programs. Longitudinal studies can track changes in conflict resolution skills over time, assess the stability of behavioral changes, and explore the broader impacts of these skills on academic achievement, social relationships, and emotional well-being.

Program Evaluations

Evaluating the conflict resolution education program, including the curriculum, delivery methods, and educator training, can help identify strengths and weaknesses. This comprehensive evaluation can involve reviewing program materials, assessing educator competencies in teaching conflict resolution, and measuring program fidelity.

Evaluating conflict resolution education requires a comprehensive approach that combines various tools and techniques to capture the multifaceted nature of conflict resolution skills. By employing these methods, educators and researchers can gain valuable insights into the effectiveness of conflict resolution education and identify opportunities for enhancing these crucial programs.

Global Conflict Resolution Education

Global conflict resolution education offers a rich tapestry of approaches and practices from which valuable lessons can be drawn. Around the world, diverse cultures and societies have developed unique strategies for teaching conflict resolution, reflecting their specific historical, social, and cultural contexts. By examining and learning from these international models, educators can enrich conflict resolution curricula, fostering a more inclusive and practical approach to teaching these essential skills.

Nordic Approaches: Emphasis on Social-Emotional Learning

Nordic countries, renowned for their progressive educational systems, integrate conflict resolution into a broader framework of social-emotional learning (SEL). SEL programs in these countries focus on developing empathy, emotional regulation, and cooperative skills from an early age. This holistic approach addresses conflict resolution directly and builds the foundational emotional and social skills that prevent conflicts from arising. For instance, the Olweus Bullying Prevention Program has been widely implemented in Norway, emphasizing respect, community, and problem-solving skills to reduce bullying and improve the school climate.

Japanese Model: Wa and Community Harmony

In Japan, "wa" or harmony is deeply ingrained in social and educational practices. Conflict resolution education often revolves around maintaining group harmony and fostering community. This model teaches students to consider the group's well-being, encouraging self-reflection and mutual respect in resolving disputes. Techniques such as "naikan" reflection, which involves contemplating one's actions and their effects on others, teach empathy and responsibility.

Restorative Practices in New Zealand

New Zealand has pioneered the adoption of restorative practices in schools, drawing from the Maori tradition of "restorative justice." This approach focuses on healing relationships and repairing harm rather than punitive measures. Schools in New Zealand employ restorative circles and conferences that bring together those affected by conflicts to discuss the impact, express emotions, and collectively decide on how to address the harm. This model emphasizes accountability, community involvement, and the restoration of relationships.

Peace Education in Colombia

In response to decades of internal conflict, Colombia has implemented peace education programs to foster a culture of peace and reconciliation. These programs cover conflict resolution, human rights, and democracy, teaching students to resolve disputes peacefully, respect diversity, and participate actively in democratic processes. The focus is on fostering critical thinking abilities, empathy, and knowledge of social justice concerns so that students may support local efforts to promote peace in their communities.

Integrating Global Perspectives into Curriculum

Learning from these international models involves more than adopting specific practices; it requires integrating global perspectives into the conflict resolution curriculum. This can be achieved by:

- Incorporating case studies and examples from different cultural contexts to teach students about diverse approaches to conflict resolution.
- Encouraging comparative analysis, where students examine how conflicts are resolved in various societies and what underlying values and principles guide these processes.
- Facilitating exchange programs or partnerships with schools in other countries to allow students and educators to share experiences and learn from each other directly.
- Emphasizing global citizenship and intercultural competence, teaching students to appreciate cultural differences and recognize the universality of conflict and the need for peaceful resolution.

Global conflict resolution education underscores the importance of understanding and respecting diverse dispute management approaches. By drawing on international models, educators can provide students with a more comprehensive and nuanced understanding of conflict resolution, preparing them to navigate conflicts effectively in an increasingly interconnected world. This global perspective enriches the curriculum, fosters empathy and respect for diversity, and contributes to developing informed, compassionate, and engaged global citizens.

CHAPTER 14

ADVANCED NEGOTIATION TECHNIQUES

Delving into advanced strategies for educational negotiations involves moving beyond foundational communication and problem-solving skills to embrace more sophisticated techniques. These strategies are crucial for navigating complex talks about policy changes, resource allocation, or individual student needs. Advanced negotiation strategies blend psychological insights, strategic planning, and ethical considerations to achieve beneficial and equitable outcomes for all parties involved.

Interest-Based Negotiation

Interest-based negotiation focuses on understanding all parties' underlying needs, concerns, and interests rather than merely bargaining over positions. This approach encourages participants to explore a wide range of options that could satisfy the interests of all involved. For instance, when negotiating program funding, rather than simply arguing over the amount, participants would explore the fundamental goals the funding seeks to achieve, potentially identifying innovative solutions that cost-effectively meet those goals.

Strategic Questioning

Strategic questioning is a technique for uncovering more profound insights into the other party's perspective, concerns, and constraints. It involves asking open-ended questions that encourage reflection and disclosure, such as "What are your main concerns with our current proposal?" or "How could we structure this agreement to better meet your needs?" This method can reveal valuable information, enabling more creative and mutually satisfactory solutions.

BATNA and WATNA Analysis

Understanding your Worst Alternative to a Negotiated Agreement (WATNA) and Best Alternative to a Negotiated Agreement (BATNA) during agreements is critical. This analysis helps negotiators understand their position and leverage within the talks and the stakes of not reaching an agreement. By clearly articulating the best and worst outcomes if negotiations fail, parties can approach discussions with a clearer sense of their priorities and the potential consequences of various outcomes.

Nonverbal Communication and Rapport Building

Advanced negotiators are highly attuned to the role of nonverbal communication in negotiations. Body language, tone of voice, and even the negotiation setting can significantly influence the process and outcome. Building rapport with the other party through empathy, respect, and genuine interest can create a more collaborative atmosphere, making it easier to navigate difficult discussions and reach consensus.

Principled Concession-Making

Concessions are often necessary in complex negotiations. However, advanced strategies involve making moral, rather than arbitrary, concessions. This means that any concession is tied to a principle or value, such as fairness, equity, or the long-term goals of the negotiation. Principled concession-making ensures that compromises are meaningful and aligned with the overall objectives of the talks.

Bracketing

Bracketing is a technique for temporarily setting aside contentious issues to focus on areas where agreement is more likely. This can help build momentum and establish a foundation of trust and cooperation. Once several less controversial issues have been resolved, the parties may find tackling the more difficult topics easier, having established a track record of successful negotiation.

Ethical Considerations

Advanced negotiation strategies are grounded in solid ethical considerations. This involves adhering to the principles of honesty and integrity and considering the broader impact of negotiation outcomes on stakeholders who may not be directly involved in the negotiation process. Ethical negotiators are mindful of their agreements' social, educational, and community implications.

Implementing and Reviewing Agreements

Finally, advanced negotiation strategies emphasize the importance of clearly defining the terms of an agreement, establishing mechanisms for implementation, and setting up processes for ongoing review and adjustment. This ensures that agreements are reached and effectively put into action and can be adapted as circumstances change.

By incorporating these advanced strategies into educational negotiations, stakeholders can achieve more nuanced, sustainable, and mutually beneficial outcomes. These techniques underscore the complexity of negotiation processes and the value of preparation, skillful communication, and ethical conduct in achieving successful resolutions.

The Role of Technology in Enhancing Negotiation Tactics

Integrating technology into negotiation processes represents a significant shift in how negotiations are conducted, offering new avenues to enhance tactics, improve communication, and achieve better outcomes. Technology has expanded the toolkit available to negotiators, from virtual meeting platforms to data analytics and artificial intelligence (AI), enabling more informed decision-making, greater flexibility, and enhanced efficiency.

Virtual Communication Platforms

The advent of sophisticated virtual communication platforms has transformed the logistics of negotiation. These platforms facilitate negotiations across geographic barriers, allowing for real-time communication without needing physical presence. Video conferencing, instant messaging, and collaborative online workspaces enable seamless interaction, making it easier to schedule discussions, share documents, and maintain a continuous dialogue. This accessibility can accelerate the negotiation process and help maintain momentum toward an agreement.

Data Analytics

Data analytics tools empower negotiators with actionable insights derived from large volumes of data. By analyzing past negotiation outcomes, market trends, and other relevant data, negotiators can identify patterns and predict the potential impact of different negotiation strategies. This information can inform the development of negotiation proposals, helping negotiators advocate for positions supported by empirical evidence, enhancing their persuasiveness and the likelihood of successful outcomes.

247

Artificial Intelligence (AI)

Artificial intelligence (AI) tools are being utilized increasingly to forecast the other party's behavior, evaluate negotiation scenarios, and recommend the best course of action. Examples of these tools include machine learning algorithms and natural language processing. AI can quickly evaluate enormous volumes of data, providing negotiators with a thorough picture of all feasible negotiation tracks and their potential outcomes. This can be especially helpful in complicated talks when it might be challenging to determine the ramifications of various options.

Digital Contract Management

Digital contract management systems streamline the drafting, reviewing, and signing of agreements, reducing the time and resources required to finalize a negotiation. These systems can automatically flag inconsistencies, ensure compliance with legal requirements, and facilitate version control, minimizing misunderstandings and errors. By making the contract management process more efficient, negotiators can focus their efforts on the negotiation rather than administrative tasks.

Online Dispute Resolution (ODR)

ODR platforms offer an innovative approach to resolving disputes that may arise during or after negotiations. These platforms use technology to facilitate discussions, mediate disagreements, and even arbitrate decisions, providing cost-effective and accessible dispute resolution. ODR can be particularly valuable in maintaining relationships between parties by offering a neutral space to address and resolve conflicts constructively.

Blockchain for Transparency and Trust

Blockchain technology's potential to improve trust and transparency in negotiations is being investigated. By creating immutable records of talks and agreements, blockchain can provide a verifiable and secure record that can prevent disputes and foster confidence among parties. This technology can be instrumental in complex negotiations involving multiple stakeholders or in situations where the integrity of the negotiation process is paramount.

Social Media and Public Sentiment Analysis

Social media platforms and sentiment analysis tools enable negotiators to gauge public opinion and reactions to negotiation stances or outcomes. Understanding the broader social and political context can inform negotiation strategies, particularly for public-sector negotiations or high-profile private-sector deals. This awareness can guide negotiators in crafting messages and proposals that resonate with key audiences, potentially influencing the negotiation dynamics.

The role of technology in enhancing negotiation tactics is multifaceted and rapidly evolving. By leveraging these technological tools and platforms, negotiators can gain a competitive edge, fostering more strategic, informed, and efficient negotiation processes. As technology advances, its integration into negotiation practices will likely deepen, offering even more sophisticated ways to navigate the complexities of achieving consensus and resolving disputes.

Psychological Tactics in Negotiation

Psychological tactics in negotiation play a crucial role in shaping the dynamics and outcomes of negotiations. These tactics leverage understanding of human behavior, cognition, and emotion to influence the negotiation process, often in subtle but powerful ways. An in-depth look at these strategies reveals how they can facilitate agreement, overcome impasses, and achieve mutually beneficial outcomes.

One effective psychological tactic is empathy and active listening. By genuinely interested in the other side's wants, worries, and viewpoints, negotiators can establish rapport and earn their trust. This connection makes it easier to find common ground and can lead to more cooperative interactions. Active listening, where the negotiator reflects on what they have heard to confirm understanding, reassures the other party that their views are being considered, which can lower defenses and open up new avenues for agreement.

The principle of reciprocity is another powerful psychological tool. This principle suggests that people feel compelled to return favors or concessions. Negotiators can leverage reciprocity by making small concessions or offering help in areas critical to the other party, which may encourage the other party to reciprocate with concessions of their own. This tactic can create a positive negotiation climate where parties are more inclined to work towards a mutually satisfactory agreement.

Anchoring is a tactic in which the negotiator sets a reference point (the anchor) that influences the subsequent negotiation process. By presenting a first offer or a strong position early in the negotiation, the negotiator can anchor the discussion in their favor, making subsequent offers or concessions seem more acceptable. The key to effective anchoring is setting an ambitious yet plausible anchor, avoiding extremes that might be dismissed outright.

The framing effect is another psychological tactic in which the way information is presented influences decision-making. Negotiators can frame proposals regarding gains or losses, depending on what is more likely to resonate with the other party. For example, framing a proposal regarding what the other party stands to gain from accepting it can be more persuasive than focusing on what they might lose by rejecting it. This approach taps into the human tendency to avoid losses, making the framed option more appealing.

Deadlines can create a sense of urgency, pressuring parties to reach an agreement. While artificial deadlines can backfire if perceived as manipulative, genuine deadlines tied to external events or consequences can motivate parties to compromise and promptly conclude negotiations. The key is to communicate deadlines transparently, ensuring they are seen as legitimate and necessary.

Developing a reputation for impartiality and dependability is an ongoing psychological tactic. Negotiators who consistently demonstrate fairness, honor their commitments, and negotiate in good faith are more likely to be trusted and considered credible partners. This reputation can make future negotiations smoother and more productive as parties come to the table with positive expectations based on past interactions.

The decoy effect is a tactic where negotiators present an option that is not intended to be chosen but makes another option more attractive. This can involve introducing a third, less appealing option that highlights the strengths of the preferred proposal. The presence of the decoy can shift preferences toward the target option, subtly guiding the other party toward a desired outcome.

Understanding and applying these psychological tactics requires skill, ethical consideration, and a deep understanding of the context of negotiation. Although these tactics can be successful in advancing discussions, they must be applied carefully, considering equity and the possibility of long-term relationship repercussions. Effective negotiators balance psychological insight with integrity, aiming to achieve outcomes that are both successful in the short term and sustainable and beneficial for all parties involved.

Cross-Cultural Negotiation

Cross-cultural negotiation presents unique challenges and opportunities from the rich tapestry of global diversity. Successful cross-cultural negotiation requires understanding how cultural differences impact negotiation styles, preferences, and expectations. By acknowledging these differences and adopting strategies to bridge them, negotiators can navigate the complexities of international interactions more effectively, leading to mutually beneficial outcomes.

At the core of cross-cultural negotiation is recognizing that cultural norms and values shape how individuals approach negotiation. For example, building a personal relationship and trust is essential in some cultures before any business discussion occurs. In contrast, other cultures prioritize efficiency and may prefer to dive straight into negotiations without extensive preliminary social interactions. Similarly, attitudes towards conflict, time, agreements, and communication can vary significantly across cultures, influencing negotiation dynamics.

The first step in bridging these cultural divides is realizing them. This requires thorough preparation, which can involve researching the other party's cultural background, consulting with cultural experts, or engaging in cultural sensitivity training. Such preparation enables negotiators to anticipate potential misunderstandings or conflicts arising from cultural misalignments and plan strategies for addressing them.

Adopting a flexible and adaptable negotiation style is crucial in cross-cultural settings. Negotiators should be prepared to adjust their communication style, pace of negotiation, and even their expectations to accommodate cultural differences. This flexibility can involve being more patient in cultures where negotiations take longer or adopting a more formal or informal tone as appropriate.

The goal is to create an environment where all parties feel respected and understood, facilitating open and productive dialogue.

Active listening and empathy play significant roles in cross-cultural negotiation. By actively listening to the other party, negotiators can pick up on subtle cues and implicit messages that may not be directly articulated, given that some cultures rely heavily on non-verbal or indirect forms of expression. Demonstrating empathy towards the other party's perspective and constraints can also help build rapport and find common ground, even when cultural differences are pronounced.

Language barriers often accompany cross-cultural negotiations, adding another layer of complexity. Employing professional interpreters or translators can help ensure that communication is clear and accurate. However, it's also essential for negotiators to be aware of the nuances lost or gained in translation and to clarify any ambiguities that may arise.

Finding shared values or goals can help bridge cultural differences by focusing on common interests that transcend cultural boundaries. Identifying these shared objectives provides a solid foundation for negotiation and reinforces the idea that, despite cultural differences, all parties are working towards a mutual goal.

Finally, respecting cultural norms and practices is fundamental to successful cross-cultural negotiation. This can include small gestures like using correct titles and forms of address, being mindful of cultural taboos, or adhering to local customs regarding gift-giving or dining. Demonstrating cultural respect can go a long way in building goodwill and facilitating smoother negotiations.

Cross-cultural negotiation, with its inherent challenges, also offers the potential for rich learning experiences and the opportunity to forge strong international relationships. By approaching these negotiations with an open mind, a willingness to learn, and a commitment to understanding and bridging cultural differences, negotiators can navigate the complexities of cross-cultural interactions and achieve respectful, equitable, and beneficial outcomes for all parties involved.

Simulating Real-world Negotiations

Simulating real-world negotiations in the classroom offers a dynamic and engaging way to teach students valuable negotiation skills. Through simulations, students can explore the complexities of negotiation, experiment with different strategies, and learn from their successes and challenges in a controlled environment. These exercises mirror the nuances of real-world negotiations, providing practical experience that students can apply in various contexts throughout their lives.

Educators can draw from various scenarios to create practical negotiation simulations, from international diplomacy to local community disputes or business negotiations. The key is to select relevant and challenging scenarios accessible to students' levels of understanding and experience. Each simulation should have clearly defined objectives, roles, and constraints to guide student participation and ensure the exercise is focused and productive.

One approach is to base simulations on current events or historical conflicts, allowing students to role-play as critical stakeholders or negotiators. This brings the negotiation to life and deepens students' understanding of the issues at stake. For example, students might negotiate a peace treaty between conflicting countries, a business merger between companies, or a community action plan to address a local environmental issue.

Preparation is crucial for both educators and students. Educators need to provide background information, define the simulation parameters, and offer training in specific negotiation techniques.

Students should research their roles, understand the interests and objectives of the parties they represent, and develop a strategy for the negotiation.

During the simulation, educators can observe and occasionally intervene to introduce new information or challenges, simulating the unpredictability of real-world negotiations. This can help students learn to adapt their strategies to changing circumstances, an essential skill in effective negotiation.

Debriefing after the simulation is an essential step. This is when students reflect on the negotiation process, discuss effective or ineffective strategies, and consider how different approaches might have led to different outcomes. Educators can guide this discussion, highlighting key learning points and connecting the simulation experience to broader concepts in negotiation theory and practice.

To enhance the realism of the simulation, educators can incorporate technology, such as video conferencing tools for remote negotiations or online platforms for document sharing and communication. This reflects the modern context in which many real-world talks occur and helps students develop digital communication and collaboration skills.

Furthermore, inviting guest speakers with real-world negotiation experience can enrich the simulation experience. These experts can offer insights into their negotiation processes, share stories from their own experiences, and provide feedback on students' performance in the simulations.

Simulations can also be designed to include multiple rounds or phases, allowing students to iterate on their negotiation strategies based on feedback and outcomes from earlier rounds. This iterative process can help students develop a deeper understanding of negotiation dynamics and improve their skills.

Integrating real-world negotiation simulations into the classroom is a powerful way to teach students about the art and science of negotiation. By participating in simulated negotiations, students can gain the critical thinking, communication, and interpersonal skills necessary for success in personal and professional contexts. Through reflection and feedback, students can gain insights into their negotiation styles and learn how to navigate conflicts more effectively, preparing them for the complexities of the real world.

Learning from the Field

Learning from real-life examples can be one of the best ways to understand complex negotiations. Let's dive into some case studies from various fields that show how tricky negotiations can be managed successfully.

Case Study 1: The Business Merger

Two big companies wanted to merge. This was a massive deal because both companies were worth a lot and had been competitors for years. The main challenge was agreeing on who would be in charge of the new company and how shares would be divided among the existing owners. Through lots of discussions, they focused on what both companies could achieve together that they couldn't do alone, like entering new markets and saving costs by sharing resources. Ultimately, they agreed to have a shared leadership team from both companies and a fair division of shares based on the value each company brought to the merger.

Case Study 2: Environmental Agreement

A mining company wanted to start a new project, but local communities and environmental groups were against it because it could harm the environment. The situation appeared hopeless until the business decided to fund community development and environmental preservation initiatives. They met with community leaders and environmental experts to understand their concerns and find common ground. The company agreed to strict ecological safeguards and to fund community projects like schools and healthcare facilities. This negotiation showed how listening and addressing the concerns of all parties can lead to a solution that benefits everyone.

Case Study 3: International Trade Agreement

Countries often negotiate agreements to decide how much they will charge each other for buying and selling goods. One such negotiation involved two countries arguing over taxes on agricultural products. Farmers in both countries were worried about being mistreated. Negotiators had to find a balance that protected local farmers and allowed trade between the countries. They decided to gradually lower taxes over several years, giving farmers time to adjust. They also agreed on measures to support farmers adapting to the new market conditions.

Case Study 4: Labor Dispute

A large hospital faced a strike because nurses felt underpaid and overworked. The negotiation was tense because the hospital was worried about costs, and the nurses were stressed and tired. By bringing in a mediator, both sides could calmly discuss their issues. The hospital agreed to hire more nurses to reduce work hours and gradually raise salaries. In return, the nurses decided to participate in committees to improve hospital operations and patient care. This instance highlights the value of candid communication and resolving disputes by addressing their underlying causes.

Case Study 5: School Policy Change

A school changed its uniform policy, causing upset among students and parents who liked the old uniforms. The school board initially announced the change without seeking input, leading to protests.

Realizing their mistake, the school board invited representatives from the student body and parent groups to discuss the issue. Together, they agreed on a transition period where both old and new uniforms could be worn, and the school offered financial assistance to families concerned about the cost of new uniforms. This negotiation highlighted the value of involving all stakeholders in initial decisions.

These case studies illustrate that successful negotiation often involves understanding the concerns of all parties, open communication, creative problem-solving, and a willingness to compromise. By learning from these examples, anyone can improve their skills and approach complex negotiations more confidently.

Future Directions in Negotiation Techniques and Education

Looking ahead, how we learn about and practice negotiation is set to change in exciting ways. As the world becomes more connected and our problems more complex, new negotiation techniques and ways of teaching negotiation are emerging. Here's a glimpse into the future of negotiation techniques and education.

Technology's Growing Role

Technology is changing how we negotiate, and this trend will only grow. Imagine using virtual reality to practice negotiation in lifelike scenarios without leaving your classroom or home. Artificial intelligence could offer advice on improving your negotiation skills by analyzing your practice sessions. Online platforms will make learning from global negotiators and sharing tips and stories easier.

Learning from Different Cultures

As people from different parts of the world work together more, understanding how culture affects negotiation will become even more critical. More education programs will focus on cross-cultural negotiation, teaching us how to respect and understand people who see the world differently. This knowledge will help prevent misunderstandings and build more robust agreements between people from diverse backgrounds.

Emphasis on Emotional Intelligence

Negotiation isn't just about making deals; it's also about understanding emotions—yours and the other person's. Future negotiation training will emphasize emotional intelligence, teaching us how to manage our feelings and better read others' emotions. This will help negotiators create a positive atmosphere, even in tough discussions, and find solutions that make everyone feel respected and understood.

Collaborative Negotiation Over Competition

The idea of negotiation being a battle is becoming outdated. Conversation is increasingly seen as a collaborative process where everyone works together to find solutions that benefit all sides. This approach will become a key focus in negotiation education, with new techniques emphasizing cooperation, creative problem-solving, and building long-term relationships.

Ethics Front and Center

Ethical considerations will take center stage as negotiations touch on more significant global issues, like environmental protection and social justice. Negotiators will need to consider how their decisions affect their immediate goals, the wider community, and future generations. Education programs will teach not only how to negotiate effectively but also how to do so ethically, making sure that outcomes are fair and responsible.

Lifelong Learning

It is always possible to improve in negotiating, regardless of experience level. In the future, there will be more opportunities for lifelong learning in negotiation, from online courses and webinars to interactive workshops and conferences. People will continue learning new negotiation strategies and techniques throughout their careers, adapting to new challenges and opportunities as they arise.

Customized Learning Paths

With advancements in technology and education, learning how to negotiate will become more personalized. People can choose learning paths that match their interests, needs, and schedules. Whether you're a business leader, a community organizer, or just someone looking to improve your everyday communication, you'll find

The future of negotiation techniques and education looks bright, with technology, emotional intelligence, cultural understanding, and ethics playing more prominent roles. In the future, negotiators will be more capable of managing the difficulties our globalized society presents. They will be able to make judgments that are not only wise but also compassionate and accountable.

CHAPTER 15

CREATING A CULTURE OF PEACE AND UNDERSTANDING

A transformative strategy, peace education aims to provide people with the knowledge, abilities, and attitudes they need to advance peace in the world, their communities, and within themselves. It's grounded in principles emphasizing the interconnectedness of respect, understanding, and compassion in resolving conflicts and building harmonious societies.

Central to peace education is the principle of non-violence, advocating for peaceful conflict resolution strategies that eschew aggression in favor of dialogue and understanding. This principle encourages individuals to explore non-violent communication methods, fostering empathy and actively listening to differing viewpoints to find common ground.

Equity and justice form another cornerstone, recognizing that peace is not merely the absence of conflict but also the presence of fair conditions for all. Peace education emphasizes understanding and addressing the root causes of conflicts, including inequality, discrimination, and injustice, and promotes actions that lead to a more just and equitable world.

Global citizenship is integral to peace education, fostering a sense of belonging to a shared humanity. It encourages individuals to consider the international implications of their actions and work towards solutions that benefit their local communities and the wider world. This global perspective is coupled with a commitment to environmental stewardship, recognizing the critical role of sustainable living in peacebuilding.

Empowerment through education is a critical practice in peace education. It seeks to equip people with the capacity to engage in critical social analysis, make wise judgments, and take positive steps toward achieving peace. This involves interactive and participatory learning experiences that inspire creativity and problem-solving.

In practice, peace education is implemented through curricula that integrate these principles into various subjects, extracurricular activities that promote peace and understanding, and community engagement projects that provide practical experiences in peacebuilding.

By grounding itself in these principles and practices, peace education endeavors to cultivate a culture of peace where individuals are equipped to contribute positively to their communities and the global society, fostering a more peaceful, just, and sustainable world.

Role-playing and Simulations

Role-playing and simulations stand out as dynamic educational tools, especially in the context of peace education. By engaging students in realistic scenarios that mimic global conflicts, social injustices, or community disputes, these methods do more than convey information; they immerse students in the complexities of real-world peacebuilding efforts. This experiential learning approach fosters a deep understanding of the nuances of conflict resolution, empathy, cooperation, and the challenges of achieving lasting peace.

In a typical role-playing exercise, students assume the roles of various stakeholders in a conflict, such as politicians, activists, community members, or international mediators. This immersive experience compels them to view the situation from multiple perspectives, encouraging empathy and critical thinking. For instance, a simulation might involve negotiating peace in a fictional conflict zone, requiring students to understand the historical, cultural, and socio-political factors. Through this, they learn the importance of dialogue, negotiation, and compromise in resolving conflicts.

Simulations, however, can recreate complex peacebuilding initiatives on a broader scale. Students might simulate a United Nations peacekeeping mission, where they must navigate international laws, coordinate humanitarian aid, and engage in diplomacy to stabilize a conflict-ridden region. These simulations teach students about the interdependence of nations and the collaborative efforts needed to build peace.

Both role-playing and simulations offer the advantage of learning by doing. They provide a safe space for students to experiment with different conflict resolution strategies and see the immediate consequences of their actions. By allowing students to experience the difficulties and successes of peacebuilding firsthand, this experiential learning method increases student engagement and retention.

Moreover, these methods cultivate essential life skills such as leadership, teamwork, and effective communication. Students who actively engage in these exercises gain a sense of agency, responsibility, and awareness of their role in fostering peace inside and outside their communities. Peace education empowers students to envision and work towards a more peaceful world through role-playing and simulations, equipped with the knowledge and skills to make a difference.

Empathy and Service Learning

Vital educational elements that promote a close bond and mutual understanding between students and their communities include empathy and service learning. By emphasizing empathy, educators encourage students to see the world from others' perspectives, nurturing a compassionate approach to addressing community needs. Service learning offers a helpful framework for using this empathy in real-world situations by fusing academic study with volunteer activity.

Projects for service learning aim to tackle particular problems in the community; they might be anything from environmental preservation to helping out nearby food banks or shelters. These projects require students to work closely with community members, understand their challenges, and develop solutions that have a tangible impact. This direct engagement promotes a deeper understanding of the socio-economic and cultural factors contributing to community issues, fostering a more nuanced perspective on social justice and equity.

Through empathy-driven service learning, students learn the value of active citizenship. They realize that their actions can significantly influence the well-being of their community and that contributing to positive change is both a responsibility and an opportunity. This realization often leads to a heightened sense of agency and self-efficacy among students, empowering them to take initiative and lead projects that make a difference.

Additionally, service learning initiatives allow students to hone various abilities, such as effective communication, problem-solving, collaboration, and critical thinking. These abilities are essential for succeeding academically and handling the challenges of the contemporary world. Additionally, by working collaboratively with peers, community members, and organizations, students experience the power of collective action in achieving goals, highlighting the importance of collaboration in community development.

Significantly, empathy and service learning also contribute to bridging divides within communities. These initiatives can remove barriers of bias or misunderstanding by uniting people with different origins and viewpoints to work toward a similar objective. Students learn to appreciate the diversity within their community, recognizing that each person's experiences and contributions are valuable to the collective well-being.

Integrating empathy and service learning into education enriches students' academic experience and prepares them to be compassionate, informed, and active participants in their communities. These approaches cultivate a culture of empathy and social responsibility, encouraging students to connect with their communities meaningfully and contribute to a more inclusive and equitable society.

Facilitating Interfaith and Intercultural Dialogues

Facilitating interfaith and intercultural dialogues is critical to fostering understanding, respect, and cooperation among diverse communities. In a world marked by increasing global interaction and multicultural societies, such dialogues are essential in overcoming prejudices, breaking down stereotypes, and preventing conflicts. These discussions allow people from different religious, cultural, and ethnic backgrounds to share their experiences, beliefs, and values, promoting a deeper mutual understanding.

The first step in leading interfaith and intercultural conversations that work is to provide a welcoming, safe space where each person is treated with dignity and respect. This setting encourages individuals to express their views openly without fear of judgment or reprisal. Ground rules emphasizing respect, active listening, and the confidentiality of shared personal stories help establish this supportive atmosphere.

It's also important to ensure representation from diverse communities in these dialogues. Diversity in participants enriches the conversation, providing a wide array of perspectives and experiences. However, tokenism can be prevented by ensuring everyone has an equal opportunity to contribute to the discussion.

Preparation is vital to productive dialogues. Participants, especially facilitators, can benefit from training or workshops on intercultural communication, conflict resolution, and the basics of the represented faiths and cultures. This background knowledge can help prevent misunderstandings and provide a foundation for more meaningful conversations.

Facilitators are crucial in guiding the dialogue, ensuring that discussions remain respectful and focused. They should be skilled in managing group dynamics, navigating sensitive topics, and helping participants explore common ground while acknowledging and respecting differences.

Incorporating activities that encourage personal reflection and shared experiences can enhance the effectiveness of these dialogues. Activities include storytelling, where participants share personal experiences related to their cultural or religious identity or collaborative projects that address common community concerns. These experiences can build empathy and solidarity among participants.

To extend the impact of interfaith and intercultural dialogues, it is beneficial to create ongoing opportunities for interaction and collaboration among participants. This might involve forming interfaith and intercultural councils, community service projects, or cultural exchange programs. Such initiatives can turn the understanding and connections developed during dialogues into lasting relationships and meaningful action.

Follow-up and evaluation are crucial to assessing the effectiveness of the dialogues and planning future sessions. Feedback from participants can provide insights into what worked well and what could be improved, ensuring that future dialogues continue to grow in impact.

Facilitating interfaith and intercultural dialogues does not aim to erase differences or reach agreement on all issues. Instead, the aim is to cultivate a sense of shared humanity, appreciate the richness of our diverse world, and build bridges of understanding and cooperation. By engaging in these dialogues, communities can move toward a more inclusive, respectful, and peaceful society.

Implementing Restorative Justice in School Settings

Implementing restorative justice in school settings significantly shifts from traditional disciplinary approaches towards a more holistic and healing-centered model. Restorative justice focuses on repairing harm, rebuilding relationships, and fostering a community-oriented environment where all members feel valued and understood. This method acknowledges that misbehavior or conflict presents chances for development, learning, and punishment.

The first step in implementing restorative justice involves fostering a school-wide culture that embraces its principles. This cultural shift requires commitment from all stakeholders—administrators, teachers, students, and parents—to view conflicts and wrongdoings through a lens of restoration rather than retribution. Training sessions and workshops can introduce these stakeholders to restorative practices, emphasizing empathy, accountability, and the importance of community.

Creating a restorative justice framework in schools typically involves setting up processes and practices that address misconduct and conflicts when they arise. This can include restorative circles, mediation sessions, and conferencing. Restorative circles, for example, allow all affected parties to come together in a safe, facilitated environment to discuss the incident, express feelings, and work collaboratively towards a resolution that addresses the needs of everyone involved.

Peer mediation programs can also be integral to restorative justice in schools. By teaching kids to be mediators, you may empower them to actively participate in settling disputes between their peers and develop a feeling of accountability and ownership within the school community. Peer mediators help their fellow students navigate disputes before they escalate, applying restorative principles to achieve mutual understanding and agreement.

An essential aspect of restorative justice is its focus on reintegration rather than isolation. Traditional disciplinary measures often isolate wrongdoers, potentially exacerbating feelings of alienation and resentment. On the other hand, restorative practices work to reintegrate students into the community by making sure they are aware of the consequences of their conduct and allowed to apologize. This approach helps maintain students' connections to their educational community, reducing the likelihood of repeated offenses.

The gathering and evaluation of data is essential to the application of restorative justice. Schools should track the outcomes of restorative interventions, monitoring metrics such as reductions in disciplinary referrals, improved attendance rates, and feedback from participants in restorative processes. This data can inform ongoing improvements to the restorative justice program, ensuring it effectively meets the needs of the school community.

Parent and community involvement is another crucial component. Engaging parents and community members in restorative practices reinforces that education and behavioral guidance are shared responsibilities. Workshops and information sessions can help parents understand the principles of restorative justice and how they can support these practices at home and in the community.

Implementing restorative justice in school settings represents a proactive discipline and conflict resolution approach. By emphasizing healing, accountability, and community, schools may foster a more inclusive and encouraging environment where all students can grow from their mistakes and make significant contributions to their community. This transformative approach effectively addresses misconduct and conflicts, cultivating a school culture of mutual respect and understanding.

Case Studies: Schools That Have Cultivated a Culture of Peace

Across the globe, various schools have cultivated a culture of peace, demonstrating the transformative impact of comprehensive peace education programs. These case studies highlight innovative approaches to fostering an environment where respect, understanding, and non-violence prevail.

One noteworthy instance is a public school in Costa Rica, a nation well-known for its dedication to promoting peace and abolishing its armed forces. This school integrated peace education into its curriculum across all subjects, emphasizing conflict resolution, empathy, and global citizenship. Students engage in regular peace circles, discussing international issues, personal experiences, and ways to contribute positively to their community. The school also partners with local peace organizations to provide workshops and activities, reinforcing the concepts learned in the classroom. As a result, the school has significantly decreased bullying incidents and increased student-led community service projects.

In the United States, a high school in California has adopted restorative justice practices to address conflicts and misconduct. Moving away from traditional punitive discipline methods, the school facilitates restorative circles that bring together affected parties to openly discuss the harm caused and collaboratively find ways to repair relationships. This approach has reduced suspension rates and improved the overall school climate, with students reporting feeling more connected and supported.

Another example comes from a primary school in Japan, where peace education is woven into daily activities and rituals. Emphasizing respect for all living things, students participate in mindfulness exercises, practice gratitude, and learn about different cultures and religions. The school's peace curriculum encourages students to think critically about peace and conflict on a personal and global scale. The impact is evident in the student's behavior, with increased empathy, reduced conflict, and active participation in peace-related projects.

These case studies demonstrate that by prioritizing peace education and adopting holistic approaches to teaching and learning, schools can create environments where students excel academically and develop the values and skills necessary to contribute to a more peaceful world. Through commitment, creativity, and community collaboration, these schools serve as inspiring models for cultivating a culture of peace.

Measuring the Impact and Effectiveness of Peace Education Programs

Measuring the impact and effectiveness of peace education programs is essential for understanding their value and guiding future improvements. This process involves assessing the immediate outcomes of student's attitudes and behaviors and the long-term effects on the school community and beyond. Various methods and tools are employed to gauge the success of these programs, ensuring they are making a meaningful difference in promoting peace and understanding.

Surveys and questionnaires are primary tools for collecting data on students' perspectives, attitudes towards conflict, and understanding of peace principles before and after participation in peace education programs. These instruments can highlight changes in students' ability to empathize with others, their willingness to engage in dialogue rather than aggression, and their capacity to apply conflict resolution strategies in real-life situations. Comparing pre- and post-program responses offers quantitative data on the program's impact on individual participants.

Observations of student interactions within the classroom and school environment provide qualitative insights into the program's effectiveness. Teachers and program facilitators can note changes in how students handle disagreements, cooperate with peers and contribute to a positive school climate. Increased instances of students resolving conflicts peacefully, demonstrating respect for diverse perspectives, and actively participating in community service projects are tangible indicators of a program's success.

Longitudinal studies track the lasting effects of peace education, examining whether students maintain and apply the principles they learn as they progress through their educational journey and into adulthood. These studies assess the sustainability of behavioral

271

changes and the program's influence on students' future engagement in community peacebuilding activities.

Feedback from teachers, parents, and students is invaluable for evaluating the broader impacts of peace education programs. This feedback can provide insights into how the program has influenced relationships, school culture, and community dynamics. Stories and testimonials from participants about how they've applied peace principles in various aspects of their lives further illustrate the program's reach and significance.

Measuring the impact and effectiveness of peace education programs requires a multifaceted approach, combining quantitative and qualitative data to capture the full scope of their influence. This comprehensive evaluation validates the importance of peace education. It informs the ongoing refinement and development of these vital programs, ensuring they continue to evolve and meet the needs of students and communities in fostering a more peaceful world.

CHAPTER 16

FUTURE TRENDS IN CONFLICT RESOLUTION

Emerging technologies are dramatically reshaping conflict resolution, offering new tools and platforms that can enhance efforts to mediate disputes and foster peace. On the one hand, social media and digital communication platforms, while connecting individuals globally, have also facilitated the rapid escalation of conflicts. The anonymity and distance these platforms provide can sometimes lead to intensified disputes without the traditional social cues that temper face-to-face interactions. Misinformation and echo chambers further complicate conflict resolution by reinforcing entrenched views.

On the other hand, these same technologies present unprecedented opportunities for innovative conflict resolution strategies. Early warning indicators of conflict escalation on social media are starting to be recognized by artificial intelligence (AI) and machine learning, providing opportunities for prompt interventions. Online mediation services and virtual reality simulations provide new conflict resolution training and practice venues, transcending geographical limitations. Furthermore, social media itself, when leveraged with intentionality, can serve as a powerful tool for dialogue and understanding, connecting diverse communities and promoting empathy across divides.

As emerging technologies evolve, their thoughtful application promises to enhance traditional conflict resolution methods, offering scalable, accessible, and practical tools for building peace in increasingly complex social landscapes.

The Evolving Landscape of Social Media Conflicts and Resolution Strategies

The landscape of social media conflicts and their resolution is rapidly evolving, paralleling the expansion of digital communication into nearly every aspect of our lives. While fostering global connections, social media platforms have also become arenas for conflicts that can escalate quickly due to anonymity, viral misinformation, and the ease of mobilizing like-minded groups. However, these platforms are not just battlegrounds but also innovative spaces for conflict resolution.

Efforts to manage social media disputes are increasingly sophisticated, utilizing the platforms' technologies. Algorithms and moderation policies aim to detect and mitigate conflict early, while features like warning prompts on potentially harmful replies introduce a moment of reflection before escalation. Beyond platform-based interventions, there are growing initiatives leveraging social media's reach for peacebuilding. Online forums and campaigns strive to bridge divides, encouraging dialogue and empathy across disparate communities.

Emerging digital tools designed specifically for conflict resolution on social media offer promising avenues for de-escalation. Apps facilitating mediation and platforms providing conflict resolution training are examples of how technology is harnessed to encourage positive interactions. This evolving landscape highlights the potential of social media not only as a source of conflict and a powerful tool for fostering understanding and reconciliation in the digital age.

Innovations in Restorative Justice Practices

Innovations in restorative justice practices are transforming how communities, schools, and the criminal justice system address conflicts and misconduct. These practices focus on healing the harm caused by wrongdoing, reconciling relationships, and reintegrating offenders into the community. By prioritizing dialogue, accountability, and restitution over punitive measures, restorative justice seeks to achieve more meaningful and lasting resolutions.

One significant innovation is the integration of restorative justice into school disciplinary policies. Traditional punitive approaches often fail to address the root causes of misbehavior or to repair the harm done. Schools adopting restorative practices use circles, conferences, and mediation to involve all affected parties—victims, offenders, and community members—in the resolution process. This approach has reduced suspensions, improved school climate, and increased student engagement.

Restorative justice programs are expanding beyond juvenile offenders to include adult cases in the criminal justice system. Programs for victim-offender mediation give victims an opportunity to discuss the effects of the crime and give criminals a chance to own up to their mistakes. This direct dialogue can profoundly heal victims and motivate offenders to make amends, leading to lower recidivism rates.

Additionally, technology is contributing to the advancement of restorative justice techniques. Online platforms facilitate virtual restorative circles and mediations, making these processes more accessible and allowing broader community participation. Apps and software help manage cases, track outcomes, and provide resources for facilitators and participants. These technological tools are precious in reaching remote or underserved populations.

Community-based restorative justice initiatives are another area of innovation. These programs engage community members in addressing local issues, from minor disputes to serious crimes, through restorative practices. These initiatives foster a collective sense of responsibility for maintaining peace and addressing harm by involving the community in the resolution process.

Finally, interdisciplinary approaches enrich restorative justice practices. By integrating insights from psychology, social work, and education, practitioners are developing more holistic approaches to healing and rehabilitation. These approaches recognize the complex social, emotional, and psychological needs of both victims and offenders and aim to address these needs as part of the therapeutic process.

These developments in restorative justice techniques are a reflection of a growing understanding of the drawbacks of conventional punitive strategies as well as the possibility of more humane, productive ways to settle disputes and deal with misconduct. As these practices evolve, they offer hope for more just, peaceful, and resilient communities.

The Role of Artificial Intelligence in Mediating Conflicts

The role of artificial intelligence (AI) in mediating conflicts is a burgeoning field that promises to revolutionize how disputes are resolved across various domains, from customer service to international diplomacy. Through sophisticated algorithms and machine learning, AI technologies are being developed to assist in identifying, managing, and resolving conflicts more efficiently than traditional methods.

AI mediation tools can analyze vast amounts of data to detect underlying patterns and triggers of conflicts, often identifying potential disputes before they escalate. By processing historical conflict resolution data, AI systems can suggest optimal strategies tailored to the specific nature of each dispute. For instance, in customer service, AI chatbots are already used to resolve simple conflicts by understanding customer issues and offering solutions based on company policies and past resolutions.

Moreover, AI's capability to remain neutral and unbiased introduces a unique advantage in conflict mediation. It can objectively assess situations unaffected by human emotions or prejudices, which might lead to more fair and balanced resolutions. However, the human touch remains crucial, especially in complex or sensitive conflicts that require empathy, a deep understanding of cultural contexts, and moral judgment—areas where AI has yet to match human capabilities.

As AI technology continues to evolve, its integration with human-led mediation efforts could offer powerful hybrid approaches. These approaches combine AI's efficiency and data-processing capabilities with the irreplaceable depth of human understanding and empathy. This partnership could significantly enhance the effectiveness of conflict resolution strategies.

Global Trends in Education

As the digital landscape transforms interactions and societal dynamics, education systems worldwide are pivoting to prepare students for emerging conflicts characterized by technological advancements and global interconnectedness. Introducing digital literacy into curricula is a crucial trend to equip students with the knowledge to navigate online environments responsibly. This includes understanding the ethical implications of their actions online and developing skills to resolve digital disputes effectively.

Simultaneously, there's an increasing emphasis on global citizenship education. This method builds a sense of responsibility for discovering sustainable solutions by getting students to think critically about global challenges including inequality, climate change, and resource access. By incorporating these themes, education aims to cultivate empathetic leaders capable of addressing complex, global challenges through informed, collaborative efforts.

Moreover, integrating collaborative problem-solving and conflict-resolution skills into educational programs is becoming more prevalent. Students practice negotiating and mediating through practical exercises and simulations, honing their ability to manage disputes constructively.

Educational institutions also increasingly adopt interdisciplinary approaches, blending science, technology, humanities, and arts to provide a comprehensive conflict perspective. This holistic education model prepares students to approach future challenges with creativity, empathy, and a deep understanding of the multifaceted nature of global conflicts.

The Future of Conflict Resolution Training for Educators and Students

The future of conflict resolution training for educators and students is poised for significant evolution. Technological advancements, a growing understanding of emotional intelligence, and the global shift toward inclusive and collaborative learning environments will shape it. As society grapples with complex social, environmental, and technological challenges, the demand for practical conflict resolution skills will escalate, necessitating innovative approaches in educational settings.

For educators, training emphasizes the mechanics of mediating disputes and the importance of fostering a classroom culture that prioritizes empathy, active listening, and mutual respect. Professional development programs will incorporate the latest research in psychology and communication to equip teachers with strategies for nurturing these skills in students. Additionally, simulation technologies, including virtual reality, will enable educators to practice conflict resolution in diverse, controlled scenarios, enhancing their preparedness for real-life situations.

On the other hand, students will benefit from curricula that integrate conflict resolution training into daily learning. Digital tools and platforms will offer personalized learning experiences, using interactive games and simulations to teach negotiation, problem-solving, and emotional regulation. Peer mediation programs will expand, empowering students to take active roles in maintaining a peaceful school environment. These initiatives will address conflicts as they arise and build a foundation for long-term social and emotional growth.

Furthermore, the increasing emphasis on global citizenship will drive the inclusion of cross-cultural conflict resolution training. Educators and students will explore global issues and diverse perspectives, preparing them to navigate conflicts in an increasingly interconnected world. Collaborative international projects and virtual exchange programs will provide practical opportunities for applying conflict resolution skills across cultural boundaries.

Incorporating artificial intelligence and machine learning, future training programs could offer predictive insights into conflict dynamics, personalized learning paths, and real-time feedback, significantly enhancing the effectiveness of conflict resolution education.

Overall, the future of conflict resolution training for educators and students promises a more integrated, technology-enhanced, and globally oriented-approach. By educating educators and students to address conflicts constructively, education systems will contribute to developing more peaceful, understanding, and resilient communities.

Anticipating Challenges

As schools look towards the future, anticipating and preparing for tomorrow's conflicts is crucial. Emerging challenges such as cyberbullying, online privacy concerns, and the impact of artificial intelligence on student behavior and learning environments demand a proactive approach to conflict resolution. The digital realm, a central aspect of many students' lives, presents new arenas for disputes, requiring educators to develop digital literacy and online conflict management skills.

Additionally, while enriching, the increasing cultural diversity in schools also brings the potential for misunderstandings and conflicts arising from differing cultural norms and values. Schools must foster an environment of inclusivity and respect, equipping staff and students with cross-cultural communication skills to navigate these challenges effectively.

Environmental issues and social justice movements also influence student activism, leading to passionate debates within school communities. Educators need to be prepared to facilitate constructive dialogue around these sensitive topics and ensure that all voices are heard and respected.

To address these evolving challenges, schools must invest in comprehensive conflict resolution training for educators, incorporate conflict resolution education into the curriculum, and create policies that reflect the changing dynamics of student interactions. By doing this, schools can provide kids the tools they need to handle the conflicts of the future and create a more secure and welcoming learning environment for all.

CONCLUSION

As we conclude this exploration of conflict resolution in diverse spheres, from educational settings to the digital realm, it's evident that the landscape of conflict and its resolution is ever-evolving. The book has traversed through innovative practices in peace education, the role of emerging technologies, and the significance of preparing for future conflicts. It underscores the necessity of fostering empathy, understanding, and communication skills among educators and students alike, highlighting that the core of effective conflict resolution lies in recognizing our shared humanity.

Cultivating peaceful and inclusive communities requires a commitment to continuous learning and adaptation. As new challenges emerge, so too will innovative strategies to address them. Integrating technology in conflict resolution, alongside traditional practices of dialogue and empathy, offers a promising path forward.

Ultimately, this book serves as a call to action for educators, students, and all individuals committed to building a more peaceful world. By embracing the principles and practices of conflict resolution, we can navigate conflicts with compassion and wisdom, laying the groundwork for a future where understanding and cooperation triumph over division and discord.

www.ingramcontent.com/pod-product-compliance
Lightning Source LLC
Chambersburg PA
CBHW020847090426
42736CB00008B/278